THE BRITANNICA GUIDE TO
THE VISUAL AND PERFORMING ARTS

THE HISTORY OF
WESTERN PAINTING

EDITED BY
VIRGINIA FORTE

Britannica
Educational Publishing

IN ASSOCIATION WITH

ROSEN
EDUCATIONAL SERVICES

Published in 2016 by Britannica Educational Publishing (a trademark of Encyclopædia Britannica, Inc.) in association with The Rosen Publishing Group, Inc. 29 East 21st Street, New York, NY 10010

Distributed exclusively by Rosen Publishing.
To see additional Britannica Educational Publishing titles, go to rosenpublishing.com.

First Edition

Britannica Educational Publishing
J. E. Luebering: Director, Core Reference Group
Anthony L. Green: Editor, Compton's by Britannica

Rosen Publishing
Hope Lourie Killcoyne: Executive Editor
Virginia Forte: Editor
Nelson Sá: Art Director
Michael Moy: Designer
Cindy Reiman: Photography Manager
Introduction and supplementary material by Barbara Krasner

Library of Congress Cataloging-in-Publication Data

The history of Western painting/Edited by Virginia Forte.—First Edition.
    pages cm.—(The Britannica guide to the visual and performing arts)
Includes bibliographical references and index.
ISBN 978-1-68048-070-2 (library bound)
1. Painting—History—Juvenile literature. I. Forte, Virginia, editor.
ND50.H57 2015
759—dc23
                                                                    2014039879

Manufactured in the United States of America

Photo credits: Cover, p. i (detail of *Haystacks at the End of Summer* by Claude Monet [1840–1926]); p. 138 DEA/G. Dagli Orti/De Agostini/Getty Images; p. ix Raphael Gaillarde/Gamma-Rapho/Getty Images; p. 3 Gonzalo Azumendi/The Image Bank/Getty Images; p. 15 Hirmer Fotoarchiv, Munich; p. 20 Courtesy of the trustees of the British Museum; p. 26 Vergina, Macedonia, Greece/Bridgeman Images; pp. 30–31 Tarquinia, Lazio, Italy/Bridgeman Images; p. 43 © DeA Picture Library/Art Resource, NY; p. 53 HIP/Art Resource, NY; p. 61 Stadtbibliothek, Trier, Germany; p. 67 Print Collector/Hulton Archive/Getty Images; p. 74 Erich Lessing/Art Resource, NY; pp. 78, 97, 131 SCALA/Art Resource, NY; p. 91 Heritage Images/Hulton Fine Art Collection/Getty Images; pp. 104–105, 107 Universal Images Group/Getty Images; pp. 110–111 Mark Harris/The Image Bank/Getty Images; p. 116 Art Resource, NY; pp. 126, 180, 195 DEA Picture Library/Getty Images; p. 133 DEA/G. Nimatallah/De Agostini/Getty Images; p. 148 Giraudon/Art Resource, NY; pp. 160–161 DEA/J. M. Zuber/De Agostini/Getty Images; p. 169 Universal History Archive/UIG/Getty Images; p. 173 © Photos. com/Jupiterimages; p. 190 Courtesy National Gallery of Art, Washington, D.C., Chester Dale Collection, 1963.10.101; p. 204 Deposited by Emanuel Hoffmann-Foundation in Kunstmuseum Basel, Switzerland, photograph by Hans Hinz; p. 209 Guy Moberly/Lonely Planet Images/Getty Images; p. 221 Andrew Burton/Getty Images; cover and interior pages graphic elements David M. Schrader/Shutterstock.com, E_K/Shutterstock.com, Valentin Agapov/Shutterstock.com, argus/Shutterstock.com, Iakov Filimonov/Shutterstock.com.

CONTENTS

CHAPTER 3

EARLY CHRISTIANITY THROUGH THE MIDDLE AGES

CHAPTER 4
PAINTING OF THE RENAISSANCE

CHAPTER 7
PAINTING IN MODERN ART 184

Painting, as it is understood as an art form, has been continuously practiced by humans for some 20,000 years. Together with other activities that may have been ritualistic in origin but have come to be designated as artistic (such as music or dance), painting was one of the earliest ways in which humans sought to express their personality as well as their emerging understanding of an existence beyond the material world. Unlike music and dance, however, examples of early forms of painting have survived to the present day. The modern eye can derive aesthetic as well as antiquarian satisfaction from the 15,000-year-old cave murals of Lascaux—some examples testify to the considerable powers of draftsmanship of these early artists. Furthermore, painting, like other arts, exhibits universal qualities that make it easy for viewers of all nations, civilizations, and cultural backgrounds to understand and appreciate.

Painting is the expression of ideas and emotions in a two-dimensional visual language.

Five hundred years after Leonardo da Vinci painted it., the *Mona Lisa* remains a pilgrimage destination to countless visitors to the Louvre museum in Paris.

The elements of this language—its shapes, lines, colours, tones, and textures—are used in various ways to produce sensations of volume, space, movement, and light on a flat surface. These elements are combined into expressive patterns in order to represent real or supernatural phenomena, to interpret a narrative theme, or to create wholly abstract visual relationships. An artist's decision to use a particular medium, as well as the choice of a particular form, is based on the sensuous qualities and the expressive possibilities and limitations of those options. The artist's choice of medium, form, and technique combine to realize a unique visual image and visual language.

Historically, the quality of a painting resides both in the technical skill of the artist as well as in the artist's ability to communicate via, and contribute to or advance, the visual language of his or her time. For art historians, decoding a visual language can provide a wealth of information about the social, political, economic, cultural, and religious landscape of the era in which a painting was made. While the historical development of painting carries out the evolvement of painting from a ritualistic to an artistic form, it also enables the development of an artistic ability to express changing reactions and approaches to world events through varying visual languages. The history of painting cannot be fully examined without the understanding that painting both expresses a worldview and defines it; that it both manifests and penetrates culture.

Western painting—signifying painting not only in Europe but also in other regions that share a European cultural tradition—is generally distinguished by its concentration on the representation of the human figure, whether in the heroic context of antiquity, the religious context of the early Christian and medieval world, or the mathematically driven context of the Renaissance. For most of its history Western painting was dominated by an accepted set of visual and thematic rules. Cultural, traditional, and religious authorities established institutions of representational painting and played a large role in the development of the craft. As artists required patronage, authorities that possessed social and economic power determined the function and subject matter of painting. Authorities engaged painting to serve their own directed purpose, from propaganda to religious practice and devotion. Painters were employed as skilled masters of a craft, providing a means to an end, rather than as individualistic creative artists.

Symbolic systems in the early history of Western painting were utilized and intellectually directed to serve the goal of traditional authorities. Their imagery had precise literary meanings, and their colour codes were intended primarily for narrative or devotional identification. These conventions developed simultaneously through the Middle Ages in what are known as the Byzantine and Romanesque traditions. The materials available to the artists of the time produce the flat visual aesthetic associated with both traditions—the quality of a painting was determined by the richness of the materials used and the skill with which they were handled, rather than complexity of composition or thematic creativity.

Gothic art—the artistic tradition that originated in mid-12th-century Europe and continued until as late as the 16th century in some areas—is defined by an increase in naturalism. It followed a stylistic evolution from stiff, simple, hieratic forms toward more relaxed and natural ones. Its scale would not grow large until the 14th century when it began to be used in the decoration of the ornamental panels behind church altars. These paintings displayed an emphasis on flowing, curving lines, minute detail, and refined decoration. Gold was often applied to the panel as a background colour. Compositions became more complex as time went on, and painters began to seek means of depicting spatial depth on a flat surface. This search would eventually lead to the mathematical mastery of perspective in the Renaissance.

Renaissance Europe in the 15th and 16th centuries provided the atmosphere in which the tradition of painting could break from its antiquated past. The Renaissance extended the tradition of figurative painting through a close examination of the natural world and an investigation of balance, harmony, and perspective in the visible world, linking painting to the developing mathematical sciences of anatomy and optics. Under these combined influences of an increased awareness of nature and a more individualistic view of man as well as a revival of classical learning, the Renaissance saw the rise of the next great development in painting.

Historical sources suggest that interest in nature, humanistic learning, and individualism were already present in the late medieval period. However, they became dominant in 15th- and 16th-century Italy as a result of such social and economic changes as the secularization of daily life, the rise of a rational money-credit economy, and greatly increased social mobility. The art of this era generated images and themes that reflected the new humanistic spirit of objective curiosity and scientific research. The artist and his patron were able to take more creative control over the content and form of the painting, and artists began to approach painting in a new way. The search for visual perfection gave rise to the idea of "art for art's sake." Mathematical formulas were developed for the perfect rendering of perspective, perception, and the scientifically correct depiction of the human body's anatomy. This freedom of artistic exploration naturally led to increased artistic expression—the artist became genius, capable of producing a masterpiece.

By the start of the 16th century, the Renaissance movement had given birth to the Protestant Reformation and an era of religious turbulence. The art of this period reflected the upheaval caused by this shift. Aptly named the Baroque, meaning irregular or distorted, European painting in the 16th century largely focused on capturing motion, drama, action, and powerful emotion. Painters employed the strong visual tools of dramatic composition, intense juxtaposition of light and dark, and emotionally provocative subject matter to evoke a feeling of disruption. Religious subjects were often portrayed in this era through its new dramatic visual language, a contrast to the reverential portrayal of religious figures in earlier traditions.

In order to capture the social upheaval surrounding Christianity and the Roman Catholic Church, many artists abandoned old standards of visual perfection from the Classical and Renaissance periods in their portrayal of religious figures. At the same time, a wider distribution of wealth in parts of Europe gave rise to a larger number of private patrons. The economic and social change was reflected by an increase of paintings by well-known artists depicting common people in scenes of mundane life. Painting presents an unusual diversity in the Baroque period, chiefly because currents of naturalism and classicism coexisted and intermingled.

By the end of the 16th century, the church's reaction to the Reformation, known as the Counter-Reformation, resurfaced the medieval concept of art and artists as servants of the church. The church's demands for simplicity, intelligibility, realism, and piety resulted in a style in Rome that was dry and prosaic. However, late-16th-century Venetian painting was little influenced by the Counter-Reformation. It would continue to develop into the typical Baroque style known as High Baroque.

The 18th century brought with it a more secular outlook as a result of the religious disillusionment fostered in the Baroque era. A social focus toward the lives of nobility and aristocracy increasingly replaced the previous religion-centric cultural norm. The Rococo style of painting originated in France and developed as a stylistic reaction to the realism and visual severity of Baroque art. The aesthetics of Rococo art are defined by light, soothing pastel colors, delicate portrayal of nature, and the depiction of aristocratic figures in luxurious garments taking part in carefree activities.

A visual response to Rococo, the artistic movement titled Neoclassicism began in the late 18th century and continued into the early 19th century. Neoclassicism and Romanticism are often grouped together in the study of art history because of their concurrent developments in the mid-18th to 19th centuries. Nevertheless both movements are highly diversified in the modes of visual representation that they utilize and encompass. They explore, largely within the realm of secularism, the classical ideal of ancient cultures. Neoclassicism represents both a reaction against the Rococo phase and, perhaps more significantly, a growing scientific interest in classical antiquity. This was the Age of Enlightenment—a time of political, social, and cultural change. In a stage of such revolution, Europe needed a model on which to base the creation of its new future. The order, calm, harmony, balance, idealization, and rationality of the Classical era is what would serve as the basis of a new social order and what Neoclassicism sought to visually express. Artists created paintings that reflected the thoughtfulness, sentimentality, and gravity of the time.

While Neoclassicism employed visual tools of classical antiquity to capture a widespread social sentimentality, Romanticism encompassed the same thoughtfulness, sentimentality, and gravity, but through an individual rather than collective response. Romanticism valued the artistic expression of emotional reaction, expressed in a visually distinct manner, over the return of Classical aesthetics. Romanticism is defined by the depiction of stirring, emotive subjects, rendered by a painterly technique that focused on the use of visible brushstrokes and dark colours that possessed an affective depth.

Development in the visual arts in the period from the second half of the 19th century to the 1960s is termed Modern. This broad classification encapsulates a wide variety of artistic thought, theories, and attitudes that reject traditional, historical, or academic forms and conventions. Modernism resides in a particular effort to create art that maintains an affinity with changing social, economic, and intellectual conditions. Nineteenth-century concerns with technique and the expressive qualities of paint handling contributed to the development of abstract painting in the 20th century, which sought to uncover and express the true nature of paint and painting through artistic techniques of action and form. During the 19th century painters in Western societies had also begun to lose secure patronage and their position of social importance. Some artists reacted to this social and economic change by holding their own exhibitions and charging entrance fees. The economic need to appeal to a broader market had replaced the demands of personal patronage, and its effect on modern art was profound.

By the late 20th century, most artists generally sought to reach their audiences though commercial galleries and public museums. They had, however, gained the freedom to invent their own visual languages and to experiment with new forms of materials and techniques that do not adhere to any set of artistic traditions or rules. Contemporary art (generally categorized as art made from the 1970s onward) is continually demarcated by the restless endeavor to extend or destroy the boundaries of expression in Western art. In the 1990s the emergence of Internet art—and more specifically digital painting—has brought on a new period of creative possibilities in which the use of computer graphics software allows for the production of virtual paintings. Each period of painting and the developments it brings builds upon the techniques, practices, and aesthetics of the past. The contemporary art critic should thus rely on a thorough knowledge of the history of painting in order to better appreciate painting of the past and grasp the cultural value of paintings produced today.

CHAPTER ONE

PREHISTORIC ORIGINS OF PAINTING

The earliest paintings in human history were the images or murals painted on the interior rock surfaces of caves in the time just before the end of the last Ice Age (15,000–10,000 BCE). Much of Europe was peopled by small bands of nomadic hunters. These hunters decorated the walls of their caves with large paintings of animals, including felines, rhinoceroses, horses, bears, and mammoths. Although most commonly associated with the prehistoric works found in France, Spain, and North Africa, cave paintings have been executed by many historical cultures and can be found in India, Central Asia, and China, among other locations.

EUROPEAN STONE AGE

Ever since the first examples of these paintings came to light in the late 19th century, they have excited admiration for their virtuosity and liveliness. The simplest figures are mere outline drawings, but the majority combine this technique with sophisticated shading and colour washes that modulate the surface and suggest the differing textures of pelts, horn, and bone. Volume is indicated by carefully controlled changes in the thickness of brushstrokes, and the astonishingly advanced draftsmanship conveys a considerable sense of movement and life. Most of the animals were originally depicted as individual figures without narrative import, and what appear to the modern observer to be sophisticated groupings of figures are, in reality, the end result of a long additive process.

As the Ice Age came to an end, it become much harder for these hunter-gatherers to live by hunting alone. Man had to modify his hunting techniques and forage for the seeds and fruits that the forests provided, or the fish and shellfish that he could find in rivers or on the coasts. Cooperation was essential, and the new situation is clearly reflected in the art of the period.

In the southern and eastern parts of what is now Spain, small bands of such hunter-gatherers left a record of their activities in the rock shelters where they camped periodically. In some ways the new paintings resemble the old. There are obvious conceptual differences between the two artistic complexes, however. These new

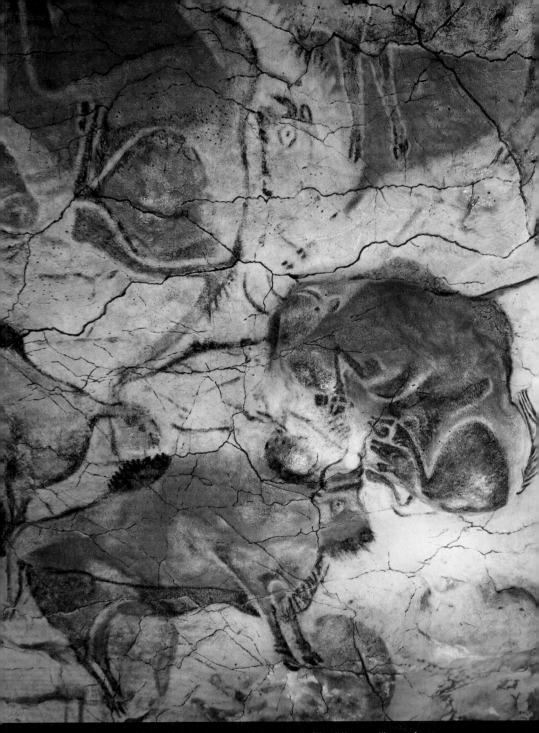

About 14,000 years ago prehistoric artists filled the ceiling of a cave near Santillana del Mar, Spain, with images of bison. Today a replica cave (shown here) and museum stand nearby.

paintings constituted the first real compositions having a clear narrative meaning, and man finally emerged as the chief actor in the dramas played out on the rock walls. At Remigia three hunters are depicted stalking a leaping ibex, while at Los Caballos a line of archers fires arrows into a small herd of panic-stricken deer, presumably driven into the ambush by beaters. Scenes of battle or groups of dancers also occur, while social status is implied in a carefully executed archer found at Santolea: he is dressed in painstakingly portrayed finery and is flanked by two other figures. This emphasis on man is new, but even more significant is the element of cooperation as part of a group whose social cohesion in warfare, hunting, or ritual was probably necessary if the group was to survive and prosper.

The subsequent Neolithic Period saw the rise of farming and the raising of domesticated livestock. This new way of life came from western Asia sometime before 6000 BCE and rapidly spread across Europe. For the first time people were able to live a relatively settled village life. While the practice of indoor wall paintings failed to make its way across the European continent, shrines at important Asiatic archaeological sites, such as Çatalhöyük in Turkey, were often embellished with ambitious decorative schemes. Excavation of the religious quarter at Çatalhöyük produced a series of shrines with wall paintings of exceptional brilliance.

THE AEGEAN AND EASTERN MEDITERRANEAN METAL AGE

The Metal Age in Europe started in the early 3rd millennium BCE, when the peoples around the Aegean Sea began to work copper, under the influence of the neighbouring peoples of western Asia. By 2500 BCE coppersmiths were also active across the Alps. Bronze began to be used in Europe at the beginning of the 2nd millennium BCE, and iron was used in Greece by the 11th century BCE and north of the Alps by the 8th century BCE.

The end of the Metal Age is usually placed at the point where written records supplement the archaeological record. In Greece and Italy this happened during the 8th century BCE or a little later, whereas in northwestern Europe the Celtic and Germanic peoples had to wait for the Roman conquests of the 1st century BCE before emerging into history. Beyond the imperial frontiers old patterns continued longer. Throughout this long period it was the Mediterranean, with its flourishing towns and cities, that produced major works of painting.

EARLY AND MIDDLE BRONZE AGE (3000–1600 BCE)

In Crete the Early Minoan peoples lived in small towns and villages with a basically agricultural economy. Although traces of their houses have been preserved, it is clear that they did not paint their walls with decorative designs. Their pottery also was at first plain or decorated with simple, arresting patterns of straight lines. It was in the period beginning around 2200 BCE when most fine vases began to be decorated with designs in white or cream paint on a dark ground. Elegant running spirals and other curvilinear motifs revolutionized the style and paved the way for the greater advances of the Middle Minoan period.

The Middle Minoan period saw the evolution of a monarchical society based on palaces situated in the most fertile districts of Crete. There were undoubtedly frescoes in these large buildings, but it is once again pottery that survived the ages and gives the best idea of contemporary aesthetics. The decorative style was a development of the previous period's curvilinear patterns in white, yellow, and red swirl around the surfaces of vases. By the end of the Middle Minoan period, the static formality of this style seemed better suited to wall decoration. It is likely that monumental frescoes from the old palaces influenced the vase painter. The combination of modeled flowers and animals with painted motifs on the vases certainly reflects similar developments in wall painting, where stucco reliefs were combined with simple painted backgrounds.

In both the Cyclades and the Greek mainland there was little interest in painted designs. Most decoration consisted of incised or impressed geometric schemes, though there were some vases with similar designs in paint. Toward the end of the Middle Bronze Age, Cretan influence was felt in both areas, and they began to be drawn into the wider cultural orbit characteristic of the following period.

LATE BRONZE AGE (1600–1100 BCE)

During the Late Bronze Age, the three separate areas of the Aegean were brought into intimate contact. Great palaces arose throughout the region. These palaces and great houses were decorated with complex frescoes whose style was based on Cretan models. Many of the figured scenes are merely decorative and depict landscapes with birds and animals or figures gathering flowers. Others show ceremonies connected with a cult or the court (such as *The Toreador Fresco*) and were probably useful in bolstering the

FRESCO PAINTING

Fresco painting is a method of painting water-based pigments on freshly applied plaster, usually on wall surfaces. The colours, which are made by grinding dry-powder pigments in pure water, dry and set with the plaster to become a permanent part of the wall. Fresco painting is ideal for making murals because it lends itself to a monumental style, is durable, and has a matte surface.

The origins of fresco painting are unknown, but it was used as early as the Minoan civilization (at Knossos on Crete) and by the ancient Romans (at Pompeii). The Italian Renaissance was the great period of fresco painting, as seen in the works of Cimabue, Giotto, Masaccio, Fra Angelico, Correggio, and many other painters from the late 13th to the mid-16th century. Michelangelo's paintings in the Sistine Chapel and Raphael's Stanza murals in the Vatican are the most famous of all frescoes. By the mid-16th century, however, the use of fresco had largely been supplanted by oil painting. The technique was briefly revived by Diego Rivera and other Mexican muralists in the first half of the 20th century and more recently by Italian artist Francesco Clemente (b. 1952).

power of the royal or priestly classes. The style is a combination of dark outline drawing, to delimit the object shown, and solid painted areas within it. On some birds and animals the feathers or pelts are imitated by slightly more impressionistic brushstrokes.

Most of these frescoes are in fragmentary condition, but a better idea of what they must once have looked like can be gained from the house walls at Akrotíri on Thera (one of the Cyclades of the southern Aegean). The wall paintings there were heavily influenced by those of Crete, both as to style and subject matter. One of the most exciting discoveries is a long frieze depicting a fleet of decorated ships sailing against a backdrop of hilly islands with towns, shepherds, and hunters scattered along the shores or set upon the forested peaks. Another painting shows a group of women at a religious festival and—in the first known instance at this period—ordinary people: two boys boxing and a fisherman proudly displaying his catch. These paintings decorated well-to-do houses.

In the great palaces of Crete and on the Greek mainland many of the scenes are more formal. At Knossos on Crete there are long lines of offering bearers in the vestibule leading to the state rooms. The throne in one ritual chamber is flanked by fresco paintings of griffins whose presence must have had a protective value. Griffins also flank the throne at Pylos in Greece, and the same site has produced fragments of another fresco showing battle scenes. Mycenae (on the Greek mainland) possesses a small sanctuary whose walls are decorated with ritual episodes, and religious ceremonies do indeed appear to have been an important part of the wall painters' repertoire. There are, however, none of the historical or annalistic scenes so characteristic of the palaces and temples of western Asia and Egypt. In particular there are no depictions of investitures or battles with accompanying inscriptions. In short Aegean paintings are far less bombastic than their Middle Eastern equivalents. This is not to say that the visitor would have been less impressed by the ruler's power in these first great European civilizations, merely that the iconographic emphases were different.

Developments also occurred in the Late Bronze Age in terms of vase painting. The light-on-dark style of Minoan pottery was by now replaced by dark-on-light ornamentation. At first (roughly 1600–1500 BCE), curvilinear patterns and simple designs of vegetation predominated. Between 1500 and about 1450 BCE, however, there flourished the Marine style, possibly the most successful of all Minoan pottery styles. Nearly every form of marine life is accurately reproduced in a riotous allover arrangement: octopuses, argonauts, dolphins, and fish, against a background of rocks and waves. Throughout the 14th century BCE, the spontaneity of the early Marine style degenerated into a rigid formality. Subsequently, Late Minoan pottery became little more than a provincial version of Mycenaean ware

In the period between 1600 and about 1350 BCE, Mycenaean pottery painting echoed Minoan. After the eclipse of Knossos, however, Minoan influence declined, and Mycenaean potters fell back on their own resources. Minoan plant and marine motifs gradually became simpler. A figure style also developed. However, unlike the classical Greeks who came later, the Mycenaean potters were not able to adapt their fresco style so as to form a convincing figure style for vases.

Finally the Cypriot pottery of the Late Bronze Age is of three main kinds: (1) a handmade ware with a glossy brown surface called base-ring ware, vases and statuettes of humans and animals being the most common examples of this type, (2) white-slip ware, in which handmade vases of a leathery appearance are decorated with patterns in black on a white slip (slip is liquid clay covering the pottery body), and (3) local imitations, made on the wheel, of imported Mycenaean pottery, which was evidently popular.

CHAPTER TWO

PAINTING IN CLASSICAL ANTIQUITY

The period today identified as classical antiquity refers to a historical period beginning during the first millennium BCE in ancient Greece and continuing until the decline of the Roman Empire in the 5th century CE. There was a large degree of Greek cultural influence in the Etruscan and later Roman world, due primarily to the Greek colonization of southern Italy in the 8th and 7th centuries BCE. Although architecture and sculptures from classical antiquity have survived to modern times, the vivid colours that historians know once decorated these works have since faded. Few examples of classical painting have survived intact except what remains of the once-grand frescoes on the walls of Etruscan tombs and the necessarily compact compositions that adorn Greek and Roman pottery and vases.

ANCIENT GREECE

At the root of Greek art was the desire to explore man and the nature of his experience. Even divine subjects were cast in terms of human behaviour, and both gods and epic heroes could at times stand as representations of and models for contemporary political achievement. This section defines the reasons for certain developments in ancient Greek painting as well as the technical advances themselves.

A major stumbling block has been the difficulty in defining the ancient Greek attitude toward art. Certainly it is clear that there was no concept of "art for art's sake" before the Hellenistic period (beginning in the 4th century BCE). Great works of art were functional: they served as gifts to the gods, monuments to the dead, or commemorations of events in the life of a city. For the first time in the history of art, painters signed their works, and both painters and sculptors explored new means of expression. The greatest sculptors sometimes wrote books detailing their philosophy of art, and there was a body of philosophical thought behind the more important advances in the painter's technique during the 5th and 4th centuries BCE.

Paintings on wall plaster, wood, and marble panels are easily eradicated, and most ancient paintings were destroyed long ago. Many fine examples, some of the highest quality, have survived, however. These are the funerary paintings on stelae (decorated stone slabs) or burial chamber walls in northern Greece and Macedonia, whose rich kings and nobles could afford the best talents from the southern cities. Contemporary vase paintings— so long as vase painting continued—often depict the same subjects and sometimes faintly reflect the style and composition of monumental frescoes, but they were in no sense accurate or even deliberate copies. The paintings on vases, now the main evidence for the development of Greek draftsmanship, were hardly mentioned by ancient writers and, although in great demand, were evidently not considered important works of art.

DARK AGES (1200-900 BCE)

During the 13th century BCE the great palatial centres of the Aegean world came to a violent end. Both internal dissension and foreign invasion seem to have played a part in this development, and, if the exact course of events is still obscure, the end result is quite clear: Greece was severely depopulated and impoverished. The small, scattered settlements that took the place of the great Mycenaean and Minoan kingdoms were not able to support the luxury arts that had flourished in the Bronze Age palaces. No wall paintings are known from this period, and the sophisticated Bronze Age aesthetics was lost. Before the end of the 11th century BCE Greece began a steady recovery, and a secure basis was laid for all future developments.

At Athens (a city that had won a position of importance in Greece only at the end of the Bronze Age) the potters invented a new painted style, which has been called the Protogeometric. Old Bronze Age shapes persisted, but they became tauter and better proportioned. In addition, the old patterns were executed with a new finesse, aided by improved equipment—a multiple brush and compasses. Using these, the painter decorated selected zones of the vase with distinctive concentric circles and semicircles, simple zigzags, and wavy lines. The vases were well potted and

Protogeometric amphora (or two-handled pot with a neck narrower than the body) from Athens, early 10th century BCE; in the Kerameikos Museum, Athens

restrained and successful in their decoration. The simple precision of their patterns is a quality that remained dominant in Greek vase painting as well as in the other arts. Other Greek cities besides Athens adopted the Protogeometric style as well.

GEOMETRIC PERIOD (c. 900–700 BCE)

The Geometric style arose in Athens about 900 BCE. It built upon the foundations of the previous period, though the area covered by painted patterns expanded and new motifs were incorporated into the painters' reper-toire. The meander, swastika, and crenellation (battlement) patterns were prominent and, together with the older concentric circles, were used by the painters to push back the large areas of solid black characteristic of Protogeo-metric vases and to create a pleasing halftone decorative effect. A few human and animal figures were introduced into this otherwise severely geometric scheme, but it was not until about 760 BCE that a renewed interest in figures became paramount.

The major achievement in this development was that of the Dipylon Master, who specialized in monumental vases used as markers over the graves of rich Athenians. These vases incorporated scenes with animal and human figures: funerals, battles, and processions as well as files of deer or goats. The figures were not conceived in realistic terms; rather, they were formalized into geometric shapes whose schematic appearance did the least possible damage to the overall decorative pattern. Nevertheless, the introduction of schemes involving figures marked the beginning of the end for the Geometric style, for later painters became more and more fascinated with this aspect of decoration, and the older pattern work languished. By the end of the 8th century BCE the figures had become much more naturalistic and were joined by floral patterns introduced from western Asia, leading to the rise of new styles in which men and gods occupied the most important positions.

ORIENTALIZING PERIOD (C. 700–625 BCE)

About 700 BCE important changes took place in vase painting. Floral motifs, animals, and monsters borrowed from the art of Syria and Phoenicia delivered the coup de grace to an already debased Geometric style. In Athens the new style is called Proto-Attic and includes, for the first time, scenes referring unambig-uously to Greece's heroic past. The exploits of Heracles, Perseus, and other heroes were painted, often on large vases used as burial containers. The bodies of men and animals were depicted in silhouette, though their heads were drawn in outline; women were drawn completely in outline. The brushwork is bold, and the general effect is monumental and impressive.

At Corinth, painting followed a different course during the 7th century BCE. Corinthian painters also borrowed "Oriental" motifs, but their predilection for small vases created a miniaturist style called Proto-Corinthian. By the end of the century human or mythological figures were rare, and the backgrounds of the animal and narrative scenes were filled with incised floral rosettes. Corinthians introduced the black-figure technique, which, although seeming to owe something to Asian influence, is essentially native to Greece. In black-figure technique figures were painted on the naturally pale clay surface of the vase in a lustrous black pigment and then incised to indicate details of anatomy and drapery. Added colours enhanced the liveliness of these scenes. The high quality of these Proto-Corinthian vases led to a flourishing export trade, and in the later 7th century BCE they were exported throughout the Mediterranean.

ARCHAIC PERIOD
(c. 625–500 BCE)

Corinth remained the leading exporter of Greek vases until about 550 BCE. The later, mass-produced vases were decorated with unambitious and stereotyped groups of animal or human figures with little or no interest in narrative. By the late 7th century BCE Athenian artists had adopted many of the stylistic features of Corinthian pots, as well as the black-figure technique. Files of animals became popular at Athens, but the artists always maintained an interest in the narrative scenes that had been so popular in the Proto-Attic style. The finest example of the marriage of Corinthian discipline and Attic invention is the François vase, produced about 570 BCE and exported to Etruria in Italy. Its surface is divided into horizontal friezes containing hundreds of carefully drawn, tiny figures showing episodes from Greek myth. The professionalism of the Attic masters contrasted with the laziness of the Corinthian painters. Unsurprisingly the Attic products soon captured the foreign markets.

The first generation of Athenian painters after 500 BCE concentrated on large-scale narrative scenes. One, Exekias, was fond of heroes. His superb draftsmanship and sense of the monumental was emphasized by exceedingly detailed use of incision to indicate the patterns on drapery, weapons, and anatomy. The Amasis Painter, on the other hand, preferred the wild cavortings of the wine god, Dionysus, and his band of drunken followers.

In general, many old conventions were retained. Men were still painted in black on the red ground of the vase; women had white

Achilles slaying Penthesilea, the queen of the Amazons, Attic blackfigure amphora signed by Exekias, *c.* 530 BCE; in the British Museum, London

skins. But some of the work of the Amasis Painter and his contemporaries used an outline technique for women and certain other figures, and it must soon have become obvious that the brush allowed greater freedom than the graver. By about 530 BCE several painters took the momentous decision to dispense with the old black-figure technique entirely and show all their figures in outline, the details being indicated only with the brush. The background of the vase was now painted solid black and the figures stood out dramatically against this sombre field. This is called the red-figure technique, and, in the hands of artists such as Euthymides and Euphronius, the style rapidly gained ground. The style made it possible to depict complicated groups of overlapping figures or incidents involving violent action.

Cities other than Athens and Corinth had studios producing black-figure vases; of these the most distinguished were in Sparta and eastern Greece. By the end of the Archaic period, however, only Athens was producing and exporting finely decorated pottery in any quantity.

Of paintings on monuments dating to the Orientalizing and Archaic periods not many survive, but a sufficient number exist to give a general idea of their form and technique. Temple models of the late Geometric and Orientalizing periods are decorated in a way that suggests that temples had paintings on their walls. The earliest reasonably well-preserved temple decoration, however, comes from the temple of Apollo at Thermon, in central Greece, and dates from the later 7th century BCE. The temple roof was decorated with a series of square terra-cotta frieze plaques, called metopes, bearing mythological scenes. Other terra-cotta plaques painted in a similar, though more developed, style have been found in Italy at Caere (where they decorate the interior walls of a temple) and on the Acropolis, at Athens, indicating that there was probably a continuous tradition in this technique.

More important, because more numerous, are the many paintings on stucco. These are found in Italy and Asia Minor, as well as in Greece. They were painted by Greeks or artists working under intense Greek influence. At Pitsa, votive plaques covered in stucco and then painted have been found. There was a flourishing school of Greek painters who decorated tombs in the colonies of southern Italy. In Asia Minor, two tombs dating from the Late Archaic period have been found near Elmalı, in ancient Lycia (now southwestern Turkey). Although depicting scenes from the life of a Lycian prince, they were certainly painted by Greeks. As on the vases, the greatest emphasis in these paintings was on finely controlled line. Colours were applied in flat, undifferentiated masses, and there was no attempt at shading, perspective, or illusionistic treatment. At Karaburun, near Elmalı, variety was introduced by the use of finely detailed motifs on the clothing of the prince, an effect closer to the work of Exekias than to the practices of the early red-figure vase painters.

CLASSICAL PERIOD
(c. 500–323 BCE)

The Classical period is deemed to have begun after Athens' double defeat of the Persian invaders in 490 and 479 BCE. By now the Archaic colour and pattern were gone from vase painting, to be replaced by sobriety and dignity. The artist's ability to render anatomy in line had reached the point where he could accurately indicate the roundness of a figure without shading. The artist was still bound, however, to a strict profile view of heads, with few frontal, and even fewer three-quarter, views of the features. The vase painters of the first quarter of the 5th century BCE included some of the finest Athens was ever to produce.

Most vase painters preferred a narrative approach, and these narratives often reflected contemporary political developments. In 510 BCE the unconstitutional rule of the Peisistratids had been overthrown in Athens. The new democratic rulers chose Theseus, an ancient king of Athens who had been credited with the union of the whole of Attica under the rule of its chief city, as a suitable patron. The vase painters responded to the general enthusiasm and civic pride by adopting Theseus as a frequent subject. This development was reflected in monumental painting. About 460 BCE the Painted Stoa at Athens was decorated with a series of paintings representing famous battles, including both legendary and historical events involving Athenians. Thus, probably for the first time in Greek history, painters placed their talents at the service of the state—moreover, a state that used them to decorate purely secular buildings.

None of the Early Classical architectural paintings has survived, but a reasonable idea of what they might have looked like may be

gleaned from the work of various vase painters who seem to have been working under
the influence of the monumental artists. The
great wall painter Polygnotus is said to have
depicted figures at different depths in his
compositional field, and similar compositions
occur in the work of the Niobid Painter. Micon
was another celebrated wall painter. Ancient
descriptions of his and Polygnotus's work
dwell on features and moods that are easy to
envisage in the light of extant contemporary
vase painting and the Olympia sculptures. The
effect of wall paintings on white plaster may
also be imagined by examining various white-
ground vases intended for the tomb, where
there is a concentration on calligraphic line
and colour applied in flat areas without any
use of shading. For all its achievements, Greek
painting was still closer to drawing than anything that might today be regarded as exhibiting true painterly qualities.

Because Greek vase painting consists
essentially of the delineation of form by line,
it could not follow monumental wall or panel
painting once the latter began to depart significantly from their common traditions. This
happened during the second half of the 5th
century BCE, and vase painting, while surviving
for a time by looking to sculpture as a source
of inspiration, went into a swift decline from
about 400 BCE.

There were certainly revolutionary changes in monumental painting technique. The Athenian painter Apollodorus introduced *skiagraphia* (literally "shadow painting"), or shading technique. In its simplest form this consists of hatched areas that give the illusion of both shadow and volume. A few of the white-ground vases exhibit this technique in a discreet fashion, but its true potential comes out in the great cycle of wall paintings that decorate the small royal tomb at Vergina, in Macedonia. The paintings, executed in the 4th century BCE, represent the abduction of Persephone by Hades. The figures are defined less by an outline technique than by complicated patterns of shading and contour lines. Another technique that also may have been included within the concept of *skiagraphia* by the ancient Greeks can be found in the treatment of Persephone's drapery: the reddish pink mantle is overlaid with slabs of darker red to create realistic patterns of light and shade, and then still darker lines are used to indicate the folds.

All authorities agree that the Late Classical period (*c.* 400–323 BCE) was the high point of ancient Greek painting. Within its short span many famous artists were at work, of whom Zeuxis, Apelles, and Parrhasius were the most renowned. They appear to have added the concepts of highlighting and

Hades abducting Persephone, wall painting in the small royal tomb at Vergina, Macedonia, 4th century BCE

subtle gradations of colour. Late Classical monuments such as the Great Tomb at Leukadia, in Macedonia, suggest that one of the means at their disposal was the juxtaposition of lines of different colours to create optical fusion—in other words, a true painterly style in the modern sense of the term. Parrhasius, in contrast, was a conservative and insisted on the priority of something called linear style, which is assumed to be closer to drawing than painting. His influence has been detected in the figure of Hermes at Leukadia and in the Lion Hunt and Dionysus mosaics at Pella, also in Macedonia. In Athens, red-figure vase painting was in decline.

HELLENISTIC PERIOD (c. 323–1ST CENTURY BCE)

The Hellenistic period began with the incorporation of the Persian Empire into the Greek world, specifically with the death of Alexander the Great (323 BCE). In art history terms, however, a new relationship of painter and patron had begun slightly earlier. Apelles executed works depicting the tyrant of Sicyon and was later court painter to Alexander the Great. His career, in fact, spans the division between the two periods. The major monument for the new period is the Great Tomb at Vergina, the exact date of which should lie between the death of Philip II of Macedon, in 336 BCE, and the death of his son Philip III, in 317 BCE. The facade of the tomb is decorated with a large wall painting depicting a royal lion hunt. The background was left white, landscape being indicated by a single tree and the ground line. The figures themselves were painted in the fashion Apelles is assumed to have introduced, and there are sophisticated examples of optical fusion and light and shadow.

Very similar in style is the famous Alexander mosaic from Pompeii, almost certainly a copy of an original painting executed about the same time as that at Vergina. Apart from the interesting developments in technique discernible during the 4th century BCE, an important change in patronage and choice of subject matter occurred. The great patrons were kings and tyrants, and many paintings exalted their claims to rule. After the 4th century BCE there were few advances until the Roman period. One Demetrius of Alexandria is said to have specialized in "topographic" paintings, but the exact meaning of this word remains unclear. All other surviving Hellenistic works are of low quality.

WESTERN MEDITERRANEAN

During the Metal Age, western Mediterranean cultures had been similar at many points. The area occupied by them extended from the northwestern part of the Balkan Peninsula in the east to the Atlantic shores of the Iberian Peninsula in the west and from the coasts of what are now southern France and northwestern Italy and the top of the Adriatic in the north to a line stretching from Sicily to Gibraltar in the south. Of the earliest painting in classical antiquity, however, little remains except the frescoes on the tombs of the Etruscans.

ETRUSCAN PAINTING

During the 8th and 7th centuries BCE, the Greeks founded many colonies in southern Italy—partly to expand their trade. In the Archaic period (6th century BCE) these native settlements evolved into flourishing city-states whose culture was heavily dependent on influences from Greek art. More in the way of Etruscan painting has survived than in the case of Greek painting. The Etruscans buried their dead in large chamber tombs cut into bedrock. In many of these, the walls of the tomb chambers were covered with plaster, and lively scenes were painted on them. Although some of these frescoes show scenes from Greek mythology, the overwhelming majority depict events in the lives of the Etruscans themselves. Funeral games were very popular subjects; perhaps the best-known depictions are those on the Tomb of the Augurs at Tarquinii, with its scenes of wrestlers, dancers,

At left, a man with his servant and child; at right, an augur, from the Tomb of the Augurs at Tarquinii, Italy, 6th century BCE

musicians, and a banquet. These paintings date from the late 6th century BCE.

The Archaic period saw the gradual evolution of an Etruscan style of wall painting whose inspiration is probably to be found in the Ionian colonies of southern Italy. By the early 5th century BCE, however, the Athenian style began to predominate, and it ushered in the Classical period as well. This period saw the use of the new stylistic discoveries of mainland Greece—shading, hatching, and simple dimensional effects.

There are few surviving later classical monuments in Etruria, and they seem to add little to the style established during the 5th century BCE. It was only with the advent of Roman political and cultural influence during the Hellenistic period that an Etruscan renaissance in painting took place. The earliest examples of the new style are the Orcus tomb at Tarquinii and the Golinia tombs at Orvieto, where there is some use of chiaroscuro effects (contrasts of light and shade) as well as simpler means of shading. Tombs in Vulci and Tarquinii of the 1st century BCE carry the development of these techniques even further. In the François Tomb at Vulci there is a celebrated fresco known as the *Sacrifice of the Trojan Prisoners.* It is next to a historical scene showing wars between Etruscan and Roman princes during the Archaic period. This renewed interest in mythological or legendary equivalents of actual historical events is yet another hint that the Greek Hellenistic allegorical tradition was beginning to take hold. It may very well have been through the late Etruscans that a taste for myth allegory was imparted to the Romans at this time.

ROMAN PAINTING

During the Archaic period Rome was ruled by Etruscan and Etruscanized kings. The city's temples were built and decorated in the Etruscan manner and most features of Etruscan culture were present. When the republic was founded at the end of the 6th century

BCE, much of this Etruscan influence survived, especially the tendency to use painting for political purposes. Accounts of temple decoration during the 4th and 3rd centuries BCE mention depictions of triumphal processions.

It was to Greek artists that the Romans turned when, in the 3rd century BCE, they first came into contact with the flourishing Greek cities of southern Italy and the eastern Mediterranean. Contact was usually in the form of war, and soon Greek works of art were being brought to Rome as booty in order to decorate the temples set up as memorials to victorious campaigns. Greek artists followed the works of art as it became increasingly clear that Rome offered the best and most consistent source of patronage.

Tradition states that Demetrius, an Alexandrian "place painter" (*topographos*), was working in Rome by 164 BCE. The exact meaning of his title is problematic, but it could mean that he painted landscapes, later to become a favourite motif in the decoration of Roman houses. Some Alexandrian tombs of the 2nd century BCE do indeed represent gardens and groves as seen through colonnades or windows in the wall of the tomb chamber. This was later to become the Roman garden scene—usually set against a cool, dark background—that is found so often in the colonnades of Pompeian courtyards.

PAGAN ROMAN PAINTING

Virtually the only example of painting in Rome to have survived from before the 1st century BCE is a fragment of a historical tomb painting with scenes from the Samnite Wars, probably dating from the 3rd century BCE. At Pompeii during the 2nd century BCE the interior walls of private houses were decorated in a so-called Incrustation style; that is, the imitation in painted stucco of veneers, or *crustae* ("slabs"), of coloured marbles. But in the second half of the 1st century BCE, there suddenly appeared a brilliant series of domestic mural paintings, the aim of which was to deny the walls as solid surfaces confining the room space. This was sometimes done by covering the whole area of the walls with elaborate landscapes.

Most examples of this type of painting have been found on the back walls of the colonnades running around real gardens. The cool painted scenes would have given the illusion that an idler in this part of the house was surrounded by shrubs or groves of trees. Another type of landscape combined sacred and idyllic features and was often placed as though behind elaborate stage buildings. In later developments of this style, the pictures painted on walls were no longer thought of as scenes through a window but as real pictures hung on or inserted into a screen or woven into a tapestry.

The subjects of these paintings are for the most part drawn from Greek mythology. Some of them recall literary descriptions of famous classical Greek and Hellenistic paintings or show motifs that suggest their originals were painted on the Greek mainland or in Asia Minor. Other panel pictures present scenes from contemporary religious ritual, and a few

BOOK ILLUSTRATION IN CLASSICAL ANTIQUITY

That book illustration existed as far back as the late Hellenistic world can be inferred from some of the so-called Megarian bowls, imitations in clay of gold or silver vessels that date from the 3rd century BCE to the 1st century CE. They often bear on their exteriors scenes in relief from literary texts that are sometimes accompanied by Greek quotations. They must, in part at least, have served as models for Roman artists.

Book illustration is known to have existed in Rome comparatively early—examples include 700 pictures illustrating the early 1st-century-BCE scholar and satirist Marcus Terentius Varro's 15 books of *Hebdomades vel de imaginibus* and a portrait of Virgil prefixed to an edition of his poems.

(continued on the next page)

(continued from the previous page)

Miniatures in the codex of the *Iliad* in the Biblioteca Ambrosiana, Milan, were painted probably at the end of the 5th or beginning of the 6th century CE but reflect pictures of the 3rd, 2nd, and even 1st centuries CE, as do those of the Codex Virgilius Vaticanus in the Biblioteca Apostolica Vaticana (No. 3225), written about 400.

The tenacious influence of Greco-Roman painting can be traced clearly in the illustrations of certain early Byzantine books. A most remarkable, if aesthetically crude, mid-4th-century mosaic pavement, found in a Romano-British villa at Low Ham, Somerset, and showing scenes from the first and fourth books of the *Aeneid*, is undoubtedly based on the copybook illustrations used for some Virgilian codex.

The only Christian illuminated manuscript surviving from before the 6th century is a fragment of the Book of Judges from Quedlinburg.

show themes from Roman legend. In the case of the Roman tombs, cross- or barrel-vaulted ceilings, where preserved, normally carry out the painted decoration of the walls, showing either a lattice-like pattern or a series of small, spaced-out, figured panel pictures.

EARLY CHRISTIAN PAINTING

It is customary to distinguish early Christian painting of the West or Latin part of the late Roman Empire from the Christian painting of regions dominated by the Greek language and to consider the latter as proto-Byzantine. The Western strain of early Christian painting may be said to have ended with the collapse of the empire in the West at the end of the 5th century CE. In the East, until the 6th and even the 7th century, painting in many regions followed the paths traced by Christian painting at its beginnings.

Early Christian painting did not have a distinct existence until about the end of the 2nd century CE. Most surviving early Christian painting is funerary and emphasizes the belief (shared by Christians and pagans) in life beyond the grave. It was only in the 3rd century CE, when the idea of Judaic or Christian allegories gained legitimacy, that any real development could begin. Even so, some rather odd compromises took place: representations of Christ as the victorious Sun God or as a philosopher occur in early Christian tomb paintings.

The new elements, then, consisted not of form but of content. As the power of the church over public and private life grew, these new elements tended to gain in importance, but they never quite ousted the pagan scenes.

With the growth of Christian communities, the catacombs—underground burial places—became veritable subterranean cities, their rooms linked by corridors. Pictorial decoration of the catacombs, limited to only a few rooms, followed pagan models. Delicate lines on the ceilings and walls trace circles and squares in which decorative motifs are inserted: garlands, birds, four-legged animals, cupids, images of the seasons, and figures of ambiguous significance (pagan or Christian)—praying figures and a shepherd carrying a sheep on his shoulders, generally called "The Good Shepherd."

As early as the first half of the 3rd century, however, scenes of purely Christian meaning were added to these neutral subjects. The oldest are located in cemeteries in Rome. Stories from the Hebrew Bible are joined by stories from the Gospels. Their style and quality vary—from light in touch and charmingly elegant to some consisting of a heavier element, with a passion of expression that seems to match the aspirations of the new faith.

CHAPTER THREE

EARLY CHRISTIANITY THROUGH THE MIDDLE AGES

The beginnings of Christian art date to a period in which the religion was yet a modest and sometimes persecuted sect. The expansion of Christian beliefs were possible only after the Roman emperor Constantine the Great decreed official toleration of the religion in the year 313 CE. Christian imperialism following this decree brought the religion popularity, wealth, and converts from all classes of society. It also brought on a need for the early church to produce Christian art on a wider scale to both accommodate and educate its new members. The art of this period has roots in the classical Roman style but developed into a more simplified, symbolic artistic expression. Although this style intentionally departs from earlier naturalism, or more conventional beauty, it possesses a great power in its communicative immediacy.

EASTERN CHRISTIAN PAINTING

A new artistic centre was created in the eastern Mediterranean with the foundation in the early 4th century CE of Constantinople (modern Istanbul) on the site of Byzantium. The term "Byzantine" is normally used to identify the art of this city and of the Orthodox Christian empire that was controlled from it and that survived from 330 until its capture in 1453 by the Ottoman Turks. From the reign of Justinian I (527–565) there were relatively clear political and ecclesiastical differences between the Byzantine world and the West, and the term "Byzantine art" from this period onward broadly reflects these differences. However, in practice, the division of Mediterranean art into two polarities is not always easy to maintain, as artistic contacts were frequent and each "sector" influenced the other.

By 1460 or a short while after, the little that remained of the empire following Constantinople's fall in 1453, together with the independent Orthodox states (except Russia), was in Turkish hands. Nevertheless, painting in the Byzantine tradition continued in Greece, the western Balkans, and Bulgaria, for Orthodox Christian art was not banned by the new Muslim rulers. Indeed, works of great technical sophistication—including icons and church paintings—were still produced.

In Russia a national art of great quality saw continuous development from a Byzantine basis throughout the Middle Ages and up to the end of the 17th century, when Peter I the Great imposed Western fashions.

In general, Byzantine painters may perhaps have retained Greco-Roman traditions more faithfully than did medieval painters in the West. There is so much variation of expression in the history of Byzantine painting, however, that it would be misleading to describe it as a "style." Although because most surviving work is religious in content, Byzantine painting does have some distinctive features. Icons, or painted panels depicting holy figures, were a major item of production, and the most important churches have their walls decorated in mosaic. The range of subject matter in Byzantine works is more restricted than that of the medieval West; scenes and figures from the New Testament and the history of the early church are perhaps the most popular choices.

Byzantine painting was a highly effective Christian art, expressing a new view of the divine and a new spirituality. On the whole, Byzantine emphasis concentrated less on presenting a naturalistic narrative than on suggesting the existence of a supernatural and timeless Christian realm; painters retained the pictorial devices of classical antiquity, even if they aimed at portraying a more abstract version of the world. It has been felt that Byzantine art as a result always contains a tension between naturalistic and abstract modes of expression.

EARLY BYZANTINE PERIOD (330–717)

Until quite recently very little was known about the icons of this age, but, owing to the cleaning of several in Rome and the discovery of hundreds in the monastery of St. Catherine on Mount Sinai, much material is now available for study.

The icons in Rome represent Christian images at their most formal and monumental. The Sinai icons are more intimate, and many must have been intended for private devotions as well as church display. Among the finest are icons that represent Christ, St. Peter, and the Virgin and saints.

Illuminated manuscripts of the period were relatively few in number. Certainly very few religious or classical texts survive. Of the latter, a copy of the pharmacological treatise *De materia medica* by Pedanius Dioscorides, a Greek physician of the 1st century CE, is certainly Constantinopolitan; it was done for Juliana Anicia, the founder of the church of St. Polyeuktos, and is dated 512. A copy of the *Iliad* at Milan may perhaps have been copied and illustrated in a Byzantine scriptorium.

Of the religious manuscripts, the most important is a copy of the book of Genesis (known as the Vienna Genesis) at the Österreichische Nationalbibliothek, Vienna; other fragmentary or damaged copies of the Gospels and Genesis are housed at other museums throughout Europe. There has been dispute as to where these manuscripts were written and painted, but either Constantinople or Syria is the normal attribution.

Illuminated manuscript page from the Vienna Genesis, *c.* 6th century CE; in the Österreichische Nationalbibliothek, Vienna. Shown here are scenes from the life of Joseph as narrated in Genesis 39.

ICONOCLASTIC AGE
(717–843)

By the early 8th century so great an importance had accrued to the depiction of the saintly and divine forms that one body of opinion in the state feared the population was in danger of falling into idolatry. As a countermeasure, a decree forbidding representation of saintly or divine forms in religious art was issued, and from about 717 until 843 there reigned emperors called Iconoclasts (those who rejected images).

In spite of the ban, pictorial decoration was not in itself forbidden. The church of Ayía Sophia (literally "Divine Wisdom") at Salonika (modern Thessaloníki, Greece) was decorated under the patronage of Constantine VI (780–797); his monogram survives, and in the apse there are indications that there was a great cross like that which is preserved in the Church of St. Irene at Constantinople and which dates from the 740s. The survival of the 6th- and 7th-century figural mosaics in the church of St. Demetrius at Salonika suggests that the ban was not strictly enforced everywhere. In any case, it was strongly opposed in the monasteries. But in Constantinople the ban seems to have been universal, and religious mosaics and paintings in all the churches were removed, including all those in Hagia Sophia.

REGIONAL VARIATIONS IN EASTERN CHRISTIAN PAINTING

In several of the more remote regions of the Byzantine Empire, variations in style and technique developed in the painting of icons, frescoes and mosaics, and illuminated manuscripts. Christian painting in Georgia dates from the 4th century and shows both Eastern and Western influences, owing to the position of the region as a crossroads of trade between Europe and India. From the beginning of the 5th century, the Georgian church approved the representation of the human form in religious painting. Accordingly Georgia was not affected by the wave of iconoclasm in the 8th and 9th centuries.

Until the 9th century, mosaics—more or less Byzantine in technique and design— were frequently used in the decoration of Georgian churches. By the 11th century the entire interior of Georgian churches was usually covered with frescoes instead. In contrast to earlier mosaics, the Georgian murals did deviate somewhat from Byzantine style and iconography, notably in extensive ornamentation between individual scenes.

(continued on the next page)

(continued from the previous page)

The art of manuscript illumination flourished in Georgia from the 6th century onward, and numerous examples survive from all periods. At the end of the 10th century Byzantine influence became strong in Georgia, and until the end of the 15th century Georgian manuscripts generally followed Byzantine models. In the 16th century Persian influence from the East transformed Georgian manuscript illuminations. Ornamentation abounded, and the representation of figures and scenes was flat, decorative, and highly skillful.

The interiors of Armenian churches were adorned with frescoes and mosaics from an early period. These paintings depicted scenes from the Gospels and images of Christ, the Virgin, and saints. Surviving illuminated manuscripts from Armenia exist in an almost uninterrupted series ranging from the late 9th to the 17th century. They are executed in ornamental designs of great richness and diversity, including floral, geometric, and animal motifs painted in vivid colours.

As regards iconography, Armenian Gospel scenes follow early Christian and Byzantine models, but the Armenian painters, especially those of the medieval kingdom of Little Armenia, often displayed a marked independence and interpreted traditional formulas in a more lively or dramatic manner. Through contacts with the crusaders and the Mongols, the painters of this period became acquainted with the art of the Latin West and of the Far East, and as a result they produced richly imaginative works.

Coptic painting—namely, that of Christians living in Egypt—consists primarily of wall paintings in monasteries, the earliest foundations of which date from the 4th and 5th centuries. Stylistically, Coptic painting differs from that of pagan Egypt in its emphasis on animal and plant ornamentation; less naturalistic rendering of the human form; simplified outline, colour, and detail; and increasingly monotonous repetition of a limited number of motifs. In content, Coptic wall paintings resemble other Christian examples of the genre around the eastern Mediterranean.

Despite the 7th-century Muslim invasion of Egypt, there was no sudden break in the Coptic tradition. It was only during the later Middle Ages that specifically Coptic painting ceased as Islamic culture increasingly predominated.

MIDDLE BYZANTINE PERIOD
(843–1204)

With the return to power of the "icon lovers," as they were called, in 843, figural art once more became important in the churches. Elaborate representational decorations in mosaic were set up in the more important buildings, painted ones in the poorer. The next two or three centuries were an age of great brilliance and represent the acme of Byzantine culture. The empire's frontiers were far-flung, its wealth was enormous, and its general culture was far in advance of the rest of Europe. After the death of Basil II (976–1025), a slow decline set in.

Icons were regularly produced throughout this period. The largest number are to be found in the Sinai monastery. Others exist in various museums in Russia, where they were brought from provincial churches and monasteries for cleaning and conservation. Some of these were imported from Constantinople; one of the finest, an icon of the Virgin known as *Our Lady of Vladimir*, was painted for a Russian patron about 1130. It is of considerable importance in the history of painting, for it not only is a work of outstandingly high quality but also is in a new, more human style, anticipating the late style that flourished between 1204 and 1453. It was at this time that the cult of the icon really came into its own, partly because richer materials became rare but mostly because the interior decoration of churches changed with the introduction of the iconostasis, a partition covered in icons.

Wall paintings were important during this period, but only one decoration by trained artists in a larger building is known, namely that in the Church of St. Sophia at Ohrid, Macedonia. The majority of the scenes that survive were drawn from the Hebrew Bible. They date from about 1050. More numerous are the paintings that decorate rock-cut chapels in Cappadocia (in what is now Turkey). Some churches (such as the 10th-century Tokalı kilise in the Göreme Valley, in central Turkey) represent the best achievements in wall painting of the period.

As for illuminated manuscripts, two magnificent manuscripts of this period survive: the Paris Psalter and a book of sermons (Homilies of St. Gregory of Nazianzus), both in the Bibliothèque Nationale, Paris. The former contains 14 full-page miniatures in a grand, almost classical style, which led scholars at one time to date it to the earliest Byzantine period. The latter book represents the grandest type of Byzantine manuscript of the age. It was done for Basil I about 880. During the following centuries many illuminated psalters, octateuchs (the first eight books of the Hebrew Bible), homilies, and copies of the Gospels were produced. A few of them contain many small-scale illustrations. The most common type of Gospel book had only a few illustrated scenes or only portraits of the Evangelists. The work is usually of high quality. Some psalters contained marginal illustrations referring to contemporary events (such as the Iconoclastic Controversy).

In 1204 Constantinople was sacked by crusaders, its treasures were destroyed or dispersed, and the brilliant middle period of Byzantine art was brought to an end.

LATE BYZANTINE PERIOD (1204–1453)

Painted panels assumed a new importance in the last phase of Byzantine art. The most sophisticated work was done at Constantinople, some of it for patrons from elsewhere (notably Russia).

During this period the Russian school was the most important outgrowth of Byzantine icon painting; after the 13th century the influence of Byzantine models continued to be felt, but both Russian wall and icon painting were showing local characteristics as early as the 13th century itself. The rigid Byzantine patterns, the dark colours, and the austere lines gradually became graceful, bright, and less solemn. Novgorod's style of icon painting, for example, gradually strengthened and took shape: the severity of faces was softened, composition was simplified, the silhouette became bold and increasingly important, and the palette was lightened by bright cinnabar, snow-white, emerald-green, and lemon-yellow tones.

Icons were produced in many other places, notably at Salonika, on Mount Athos, and in many other centres in what are now the Balkan states and areas such as Russia and Ukraine. After the Turkish conquests of the mid-15th century, icons continued to be painted in large numbers in every part of the Orthodox world. In the 16th century Crete became an important centre, and many Cretan painters worked also in Venice, where there was a large Greek colony; many of the products of this school are to be found there today in the museum attached to the Church of St. George of the Greeks.

In terms of wall paintings, it is probable that artists who had fled the capital after 1204 established themselves in a number of different areas and that the earliest wall paintings of the late Byzantine period were the work of men they had trained. By the end of the century, the local art in the Byzantine Empire emerged as the regional art of Salonika. Throughout the 14th century a great deal of work was done by painters in the Balkan region, notably in Greece and Bulgaria.

In Russia the Mongol invasion about the middle of the 13th century disrupted previous centres of production, such as Kiev and Vladimir-Suzdal. Only in the northern regions of Russia—particularly in the Novgorod district—

PAINTERS OF THE LATE BYZANTINE PERIOD

Perhaps the most prominent figure in Russian painting in the late Byzantine period was Theophanes the Greek (b. *c.* 1330/40–d. 1405). He was one of the leading painters of murals, icons, and miniatures who influenced the 15th-century painting style of the Novgorod school and the Moscow school. His early career was spent in Constantinople and Crimea, but after about 1370 he worked in Russia. Although he painted hundreds of works, the only ones that can be certainly attributed to him are frescoes in the Church of the Transfiguration in Novgorod (1378).

His paintings, though closely adhering to Byzantine styles, show distinctive Russian features, notably elongated proportions and delicacy of detail. Similar characteristics and features can be seen in his Novgorod frescoes and especially in the central part of the iconostasis in the Cathedral of the Annunciation in the Moscow Kremlin.

Among the immediate followers and collaborators of Theophanes was Andrey Rublyov, whose religious types are imbued with a fresh spirituality. His best-known work

(continued on page 54)

The Old Testament Trinity, Russian icon painted by Andrey Rublyov, *c.* 1410; in the State Tretyakov Gallery, Moscow

(continued from page 52)

is the icon *The Old Testament Trinity (c. 1410)*, painted for the Trinity-St. Sergius Monastery at Sergiyev Posad. The subject—popular in Byzantine iconography—is the visit of three angels to Abraham and Sarah. But the severe symbolism of the old Byzantine tradition is transformed into something more human. It is one of the great creations of medieval Russian painting.

Another inspired Novgorod painter of the 15th century was Dionisi, whose art is marked by the extreme elongated stylizing of his figures as well as a subtle and glowing colour scheme. He and his predecessor Rublyov succeeded in expressing the aura of spirituality that is the essence of the Russian icon.

did painting continue to develop. As early as the second half of the 12th century, the city of Novgorod had developed an individual style, combining Byzantine severity with a folk-art picturesqueness. Novgorod escaped damage by the Asiatic hordes and became virtually the metropolis and cultural centre of old Rus after the fall of Kiev (1240). Together with the city of Pskov and other northwestern Russian population centres, it harboured many Greek artists, who continued to work in the traditions of Byzantium.

At Constantinople some paintings of outstanding quality were executed at the Monastery of the Chora, now known as Kariye Cami, and it is known from the texts that similar paintings existed in a number of other churches there. The same style was also introduced to Mistrás, in the Peloponnese as well as in paintings in the monasteries of the Morava Valley in Serbia done at the end of the 14th century and beginning of the 15th.

Illuminated manuscripts of the last Byzantine age are not as numerous as those of the middle period, but their quality is often just as high. A few seem to have been produced during the 13th century, both at Constantinople and in the cities where Orthodox nobles established themselves while the Latin crusaders were in possession of the capital, notably Nicaea and Trebizond. After the return to Constantinople in 1261 the noble families seem to have played a greater role than the emperors as patrons of all arts, and many of the more important works of art of the age were produced on their behalf.

Manuscripts were, of course, also copied and illuminated in the monasteries, and this process continued until printing made it obsolete. Few of the later ones contain illuminations of great quality. In the Slavic lands, however, fine work continued, and in Romania excellent manuscripts were executed in the 16th century.

POST-BYZANTINE RUSSIA

In the 15th century, major changes began to take place in Russian icon painting, leading to the birth of what may justifiably be called a national art. This evolution first became noticeable in the gradual elimination of the Mediterranean setting depicted in the background of icons. Greek basilicas with their porticoes and atria (patios or courts) were replaced by Russian churches with their cupolas and *kokoshniki* (literally "women's headdresses" but here, by extension, "gables"). Russian saints and episodes from their lives furnished subjects for the Russian artists; Muscovite types and native costumes began to appear in icon painting. The colours were extraordinarily brilliant, and there was particular emphasis on outline.

Many of the great icon and fresco painters in the 16th century worked first at Novgorod and later at Moscow, thus linking Novgorod and Moscow closely in artistic terms and in particular introducing to Moscow features characteristic of the Byzantine and Novgorodian traditions.

At the end of the 16th century the Stroganov school made its appearance in

Moscow, introducing a small-scale manner of icon painting. The masters of the Stroganov school became famous for the elegant attitudes of their figures, their Eastern choice of colours, and their elaborate detail.

Moscow icons of the 17th century constitute the last authentically Russian painting. As early as 1650 much of their Russian character had disappeared. From the end of the century, western European influences spread rapidly.

MEDIEVAL CHRISTENDOM IN WESTERN EUROPE

Ancient Roman civilization in western Europe foundered and fell apart in the second half of the 6th century CE, and the changes that took place between late antiquity and the medieval period were fundamental and catastrophic. Urban life collapsed, patronage of the arts all but ceased, and the centuries-old Mediterranean traditions of artistic training and production died out almost everywhere. It was only in a few places in Italy that artistic production continued unbroken, albeit much reduced. Increasingly, the cultural fabric of northern Europe was determined by the various tribal peoples—Franks, Vandals, Goths, Angles, and Saxons—who migrated into the western provinces of the old Roman Empire during the 4th to 6th centuries.

EARLY MIDDLE AGES

The reappearance of painting in northern Europe in the late 7th century was determined by two overriding factors. The first was the conversion of these peoples to Christianity. By the 6th century the Christian church had developed an extensive iconographic repertory, and Christian images were in use everywhere: both as icons, which functioned as focal points of worship, and as symbolic and narrative compositions, which proclaimed the mysteries of the faith and instructed the unlettered in the stories of sacred scripture. The second factor that induced the new masters of Europe to develop the art of painting and figural imagery was their fascination with—and desire to emulate— the culture of the late Roman world, in which painting had been widely employed.

Apart from a small number of images on wooden panels, two kinds of painting have survived from the early Middle Ages: large-scale painting on the walls of buildings and small-scale painting in manuscripts. These two genres involved differing techniques and constituted separate artistic traditions. Only a tiny percentage has survived of the wall paintings originally found in almost every church and in many public buildings throughout the West. Illuminated books of this period, on the other hand, have come down in large numbers. Made of resilient animal skin and protected by stout wooden boards, they last almost indefinitely and remain in a remarkably good state of preservation. Artists in the Middle Ages expended some of their greatest efforts on the illumination of the Gospels, the books of the Hebrew Bible, and the other liturgical, devotional, and instructional texts that the church required.

ROME, THE BRITISH ISLES, AND THE FRANKS (c. 600–9TH CENTURY)

Rome, the seat of the pope, was one place in the West where an unbroken tradition of artistic patronage and production endured from late antiquity into the high Middle Ages and beyond. Furthermore it is recorded that Roman missionaries, who played a major role in the conversion of England to Christianity in the early 7th century, brought painted images with them.

Another source for a significant deal of painting in the early Middle Ages was the 6th- and 7th-century monasteries in Ireland and England. In their scriptoria (writing rooms) manuscripts were written and decorated in increasingly elaborate fashion. Portraits of the Evangelists became brilliant symbols, their bodies and clothes radically abstracted and brightly coloured. The great full-page initial letters in Gospel books of the British Isles—besides articulating the text—serve as images, almost as icons, of the Word of God.

The innovations of these early Irish and English scribes and artists left a lasting imprint on the subsequent development of book decoration throughout Europe. The elaborate initial letters that are found in nearly all later decorated manuscripts were first devised in the British Isles, and the decorative vocabulary of later continental illumination owed much to English and Irish invention.

It was only in the first half of the 8th century that manuscripts began to be elaborately decorated in the Frankish kingdom (an area roughly comprising northern France and southwestern Germany as far as the Rhineland). This production is known as Merovingian, after the Frankish dynasty that ruled, in name at least, until 751. In its subject matter, early Frankish illumination is decorative and symbolic rather than narrative.

In the mid-8th century a new Frankish dynasty came to power. Under Charlemagne (who reigned from 768 to 814), a new courtly culture was created to rival those of late antique Rome and of contemporary Byzantium. The achievements of two groups of artists, members of both of which worked for the emperor and his court, were to determine the overall development of painting in northern Europe for the next three centuries. One group, the so-called Court school, produced a series of splendidly rich Gospel books. Their decoration is extremely inventive and the figures—with carefully modeled limbs issuing from dense carapaces of brilliantly coloured, elaborately folded drapery—show a completely new mastery of the human form. The second group concentrated on figures dressed in archaic white garments, with faces and limbs modeled in dramatic chiaroscuro—a conscious and very successful evocation of the painting of antiquity.

St. Mark, illuminated manuscript page from the Gospel book of the Court school of Charlemagne, *c.* 810; in the Stadtbibliothek, Trier, Germany

LATE ANGLO-SAXON ENGLAND

In England a coherent and magnificent style of book illumination was developed in the 960s in the scriptorium at Winchester. Behind this initiative in lavish book production lay a movement of religious reform, instituted by the leading churchmen of the realm and supported by the king. In the scriptoria at Glastonbury and

Canterbury a lively tradition of expressive out-line drawing developed. Some of the most arresting Anglo-Saxon works of the period are filled with animated figures in flying ruffled drapery.

OTTONIAN GERMANY

In Germany, now under the Saxon Ottonian dynasty, royal and ecclesiastical patronage also brought about a great revival in the arts. As in England, this revival followed a reform movement that touched the leading monastic communities and revitalized religious life.

Ottonian art, like Anglo-Saxon, was solidly based on earlier Carolingian invention. The dominant figure in the late 10th century was an artist known as the Master of the Registrum Gregorii, who seems to have been based at Trier. Drawing inspiration from early Christian and Carolingian manuscripts, he developed a new manner of painting, in which meticu-lously detailed, smoothly modeled figures are placed in elaborate and precisely calculated spatial settings.

In about 1000, younger contemporaries of this man produced, on royal commission, a series of magnificently illuminated books. The portraits of the Evangelists and the images in these books are remarkable for their formal subtlety and iconographic ingenuity.

During the first half of the 11th century, manuscript illumination flourished in various monastic scriptoria in Germany. At Cologne, in addition to those by the Master of the Registrum Gregorii, Eastern painted books must also have been available as models, since the wonderfully fluid painterly compositions of the early works of the school appear to have been inspired by contemporary Byzantine painting. At Regensburg the splendid house style was based largely on one grand Carolingian book, the golden Gospels of Charles the Bald, in the possession of the Abbey of St. Emmeram. In this scriptorium, illustrations became vehicles for elaborate theological arguments, laid out in complex schematic compositions and glossed with explanatory inscriptions. At Corvey, on the other hand, book illumination was ornamental and largely aniconic. The ornamentation consisted chiefly of darkly brilliant initial pages, with large gilded capital letters set on densely patterned purple grounds.

From literary sources and fragmentary remains it is known that wall painting was common in Germany during this period. But only one extensive program survives, in the Church of St. George on the island of Reichenau, in Lake Constance. This dates from the late 10th century and consists of a sequence of the miracles of Christ's ministry.

ROMANESQUE PAINTING

In the second half of the 11th century in many parts of Europe, new energies and new initiatives are apparent in painting, sculpture, and architecture. It is impossible to categorize these changes fully or to reduce them to a common denominator, but in many places there was a tendency toward greater schematization and bold configurations in design, in which strong and abstract structures of line and colour predominate. The surfaces of clothed bodies are enlivened by intricate schemes of folds and pleats and highlights in regular patterns of reiterated parallel and converging lines. These developments are partly explained by the arrival in the West of examples of recent Byzantine painting, with its elaborate patterned highlighting. Another factor seems to have been an aesthetic that defined beauty in terms of symmetry and order and the juxtaposition of pure, bright saturated colours.

ITALY

In Italy the critical role played by Byzantine art is clearest of all. It is evident both in the north and in the south, particularly at Montecassino, where Byzantine artists were summoned by the abbot Desiderius in the 1060s to work on the decoration of his new abbey church. The wall paintings commissioned by the same Desiderius at

Sant'Angelo in Formis are the outstanding surviving example of the consequent fusion of Eastern and Western traditions. In Rome and central Italy in the first decades of the century, the dominant fashion was for figures whose garments hung in a multitude of fine parallel pleats. In the 12th century Italian artists took an increasing interest in ancient Roman art.

FRANCE

An early Romanesque art emerged in scriptoria throughout France in the late 11th century. By the early 12th century, major schools of painting flourished in Burgundy, at the great Benedictine abbey of Cluny, and at the newly founded Cistercian house of Cîteaux. From Cluny there is a lectionary in which Byzantine influence is strong and a copy of St. Ildefonsus' treatise on the virginity of Mary that owes more to late Ottonian examples than to Byzantium. At Cîteaux the early manuscripts show evidence of strong Norman and English influence in their decoration and a satirical delight in observation. Later, in a group of manuscripts of the second quarter of the century, the illustrations are colour-washed drawings with slender figures whose drapery falls in parallel rounded pleats—apparently inspired by contemporary southern Italian work.

The most complete surviving set of early Romanesque wall paintings in France is in the church of Saint-Savin-sur-Gartempe, where the compositions show great narrative vigour and inventiveness. In general, wall painters in the early Middle Ages had very limited means at their disposal, and it is remarkable how skilled artists were able to deploy three or four colours to impressive and unifying effect. An example of this is at Montcherand, in the Swiss Jura, where simple hues of brown, ochre, dull blue, and white have been used to depict ecstatically disputing Apostles beneath a huge Christ in Majesty.

ENGLAND

In the 1120s in England artists at the abbey of St. Albans, drawing on earlier English traditions and Ottonian painting from Germany, devised cycles of full-page scenes with large figures set off against rectangular panels of colour. In structural density, in their use of accumulated motifs and bright areas of colour, and in the intensity of their storytelling, these images have few parallels in earlier English art.

In the second quarter of the century acquaintance with contemporary Byzantine painting—probably via illuminated manuscripts—and recent developments on the Continent led English artists to a more organic, if expressively attenuated, conception of the human body. Drapery is now stretched and gathered; faces are more heavily modeled than before; and glances and gestures are even more piercing and insistent. This is first seen about 1130 in the great Bible of the Abbey of St. Edmund at Bury. Later stages of the development can be traced in a series of magnificent manuscripts from southern English scriptoria and in one wall painting in St. Anselm's Chapel in Canterbury cathedral (1160s).

In the late 11th century in southern England and in northern France a type of initial letter emerged in which men, monsters,

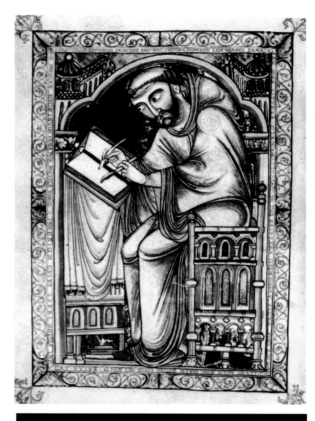

The scribe Eadwine, illuminated manuscript page from the *Eadwine Psalter, c.* 1155–60; in Trinity College, Cambridge, United Kingdom

beasts, and birds climb and struggle in "tangle-woods" of *rinceaux* (ornamental motifs consisting of sinuous and scrolling foliate branches). On the surface they are an expression of that love of joyously outlandish, grotesque, and even warring imagery that is a ubiquitous feature of 12th-century art; but at a deeper level they are concerned with man's unending conflict with sin and the Devil.

SPAIN

An extraordinary tradition of manuscript illumination evolved in Spain in the 10th and 11th centuries. The chief vehicle for this art was the commentary on the book of Revelation of Beatus of Liebana, a text that seems to have been taken by contemporaries as a symbol of Christian resistance to the Muslim Arabs who dominated much of the Iberian Peninsula in the early Middle Ages. The Arab cultural presence in Spain was all-pervasive, and—even if it did not account for the strongly patterned, sometimes barbaric compositions and for the brilliant jarring use of colour—it was responsible for particular motifs adopted by these illuminators.

Northern Spain also produced some of the most splendid Romanesque wall paintings. Spanish artists favoured formal symmetrical and hieratic compositions and strong, barely modulated colours. The human form and the stiff, banded drapery that encases it are consistently more idealized and abstracted than in other European painting of the time.

THE MEUSE VALLEY

The results of the great increase in artistic production, the sudden intensification of patronage, and the wealth of artistic invention found throughout Europe in the late 11th and early 12th century are nowhere more clear than in the valley of the Meuse, in what is now eastern Belgium. One of the leading centres of artistic production was the abbey of Stavelot. The decoration of the outstanding early manuscript from its scriptorium, the Stavelot Bible, of about 1094–97, is the work of various hands and is a perfect microcosm of the influences and interests that gave rise to the first Romanesque painting. It is a clear example of the concept of expounding a theological argument in a composition of diagrammatic complexity— something dear to the 12th century.

GERMANY AND AUSTRIA

Full-page compositions of complex iconography in elaborate formal settings are also a characteristic of north German manuscripts of the 12th century. They are found above all in a group of books associated with the all-powerful duke of Saxony Henry the Lion (1142–95) and prepared in the abbey of Helmarshausen on the Weser River.

A very different art was practiced in the southeast, where Salzburg was the leading centre. A strong Italian element is detectable in the illustrations in books of the first half of the 12th century. Manuscripts of the era demonstrate illustrations parallel to the great contemporary English books and also show a preoccupation with Byzantine models for figures and faces. But the strong Italian influence in the Salzburg scriptorium ensured that the German figures remained calmer and more solid than their exuberant English cousins. In the middle of the century a wonderfully elegant art of pen drawing emerged at Salzburg, with expressive swaying and gesticulating figures set against backgrounds of blue and green as seen in the Antiphonary of St. Peter's at Salzburg.

A number of early wall paintings survive in Austria and Germany, but many of those in Germany have suffered disastrously from over-restoration. In Austria the major monument is the late 11th-century Christological cycle in the west choir of the abbey Church at Lambach, apparently by artists from Salzburg. This work was strongly influenced by the contemporary Byzantinizing art of the Veneto region of Italy.

In Germany well-preserved paintings of the early 12th century at Idensen have strong four-square compositions and clearly contoured, stern-faced figures, which stem from late Ottonian tradition. Half a century later, on the lower Rhine, a new spirit and mentality were expressed in two splendid but drastically repainted cycles where elegantly drawn figures play against panels and frames of blue and green, illustrating recondite and complicated iconographic programs.

LATE 12TH CENTURY

In the late 12th century two broad developments took place in wall painting and manuscript illumination throughout the West. On the one hand, forms became smoother and more fluent, and a less abstract and less aggressively patterned interpretation was put on nature. On the other hand, the perennial interest that Western artists had shown in contemporary Byzantine art grew more intense, and this sometimes led to the opposite extremes of turbulent and mannered design. Both of these tendencies probably aimed at representing human actions and interactions with greater conviction and increased psychological power.

In England the new soft style becomes apparent by the late 12th century and, in some late examples, represents pure Early Gothic painting. A similar evolution can be traced in northern France, where Byzantine influence was strong. One variation, which originated in the Meuse Valley, was the so-called *Muldenfaltenstil*, named after the small, troughlike folds into which drapery breaks. In Germany this style is found in manuscripts made on the middle Rhine and at Regensburg.

The other major factor in European art about 1200 was a widespread interest in Byzantium. Byzantine mosaicists in the late 12th century undertook vast commissions in Venice and Sicily. These provided Western artists with the opportunity of studying monumental Byzantine art of the finest quality at first hand. Imported Byzantine illuminated manuscripts and panel paintings, enamels, and ivory carvings were also available as models. The purest and most striking instances of Byzantinizing painting are found in Italy.

This swirling, contrived Byzantine art of the middle to late 12th century gave rise to many experiments in northern Europe. It strongly affected artists at Salzburg and on the upper Rhine. Contemporary Byzantine art also directly inspired the *Zackenstil*—the new, early-Gothic, jagged style of early 13th-century Germany.

In the early Middle Ages, wall painters had largely been laymen, whereas the illumination of manuscripts had been practiced almost exclusively in monastic scriptoria. In the late 12th century the production of books began to be taken up by lay scribes and painters working in their own shops. At the same time, illuminated books of private devotion and both religious and secular illustrated texts became increasingly popular. This process continued in the 13th century, when growing literacy and learning among laymen and the rise of the universities created a demand for illuminated and illustrated texts of all kinds.

GOTHIC PAINTING

"Gothic" is the term generally used to denote the style of architecture, sculpture, and painting that developed from the Romanesque during the 12th century and became predominant in Europe by the middle of the 13th century. The many variations within the style are usually distinguished by the use of chronological or geographical terms.

EARLY GOTHIC

One of the moves away from Byzantine influence took the form of a softer, more realistic style whose general characteristics survived until the middle of the 13th century. In Germany, however, the graceful pictorial style did not become popular. Instead the successor to the Byzantine conventions of the 12th century was the aforementioned twisted and angular style called the *Zackenstil*. In the Soest altar (*c.* 1230–40), for example, the drapery is shaped into abrupt angular forms and often falls to a sharp point, like an icicle.

HIGH GOTHIC

Certain characteristics of high Gothic sculpture spread to influence painting about 1250–60. Probably the first place where this became evident was Paris, where Louis IX (St. Louis) was a leading patron. In an evangelary (a book containing the four Gospels) prepared for use at Louis IX's palace chapel, one can see the early Gothic pictorial style superseded quite abruptly by a drapery style

Nativity scene from the Niederwildungen altarpiece, painted by Conrad von Soest, 1403; in the Stadtkirche, Bad Wildungen, Germany

incorporating large, rather angular folds. Combined with this style was a growing emphasis on minute detail almost as an end in itself; faces, in particular, became tiny essays in virtuoso penmanship.

Although details such as faces and hands continued to be described chiefly by means of line, in a subsequent development drapery and other shapes were modeled in terms of light and shade. This "discovery of light" began around 1270–80 but is particularly associated with a well-known Parisian royal illuminator called Master Honoré. It is possible that this new use of light was stimulated by developments in Italian painting. However that may be, Italian influence emerged quite clearly in the second quarter of the 14th century, in the workshop of the Parisian artist Jean Pucelle. His painting shows an awareness of Italian iconography and of the recent Italian discovery of perspective in the portrayal of space.

The French style was introduced fairly rapidly into England. Although Henry III apparently was not a bibliophile, various manuscripts contain echoes of the dainty and minute style of Louis IX's artists. Some large-scale paintings that demonstrate similar stylistic traits survive in Westminster Abbey. Subsequent changes in English painting involved greater decorative elaboration. Although some books with elaborate border decorations date from as early as the 13th century, such decorations became much more lavish in the 14th. There are occasional indications of Italian influence but nothing comparable to that found in books from Jean Pucelle's Parisian workshop.

Italian influence reached other European countries. An Italianate style of painting developed in Spain in the 14th century and, to a lesser extent, parts of German-speaking Europe, including Austria.

ITALIAN GOTHIC

In the 13th century both Rome and Tuscany had flourishing pictorial traditions, and both, until the middle of the century, were strongly influenced by Byzantine art. The transitional period 1250–1300 is poorly documented. Since much of the Roman work was subsequently destroyed, evidence for what was happening in Rome must be sought outside the city. The most important location where such evidence exists is Assisi, where the upper church of St. Francis was decorated by Roman-trained fresco painters between about 1280 and 1300. In Tuscany the stylistic changes are probably best revealed by Duccio di Buoninsegna's Maestà altarpiece (1308–11), formerly the high altarpiece of Siena cathedral.

As with all Gothic decorative art, the changes are in the direction of greater realism. By the end of the 13th century, painters in Rome, such as Pietro Cavallini and probably Duccio in Tuscany, had discovered, like their contemporaries in Paris, the use to which light could be put in figure modeling. The Italian painters also made sudden and unexpected advances in the manipulation of perspective to describe the space of the scenes they were painting. More than this, the best painters developed an extraordinary ability to create figures that really look as if they are communicating with each other by gesture and expression.

How far the Italian tradition of painting on a large scale magnified problems such as perspective, it would be hard to say. The survival of a large-scale mural tradition certainly marks Italy off from the north. Italian mural paintings were executed with a technique involving pigment applied to, and absorbed by, lime plaster that was still fresh (hence the name of this type of painting—fresco). It was with work in this medium as much as in tempera (a substance binding powdered pigments, usually made from egg at this date) on panel that artists in Italy won their reputations. The typical subjects of fresco painting were series of biblical or hagiographic narratives, thus their Italian name: *istorie*, or "history painting."

By the middle of the 14th century, Italian painters had achieved a unique position in

Lamentation, fresco by Giotto, *c.* 1305–06; in the Arena Chapel, Padua, Italy

Europe. They had made discoveries in the art of narrative composition that set them quite apart from painters anywhere else. Their achievements in capturing reality were not easily ignored. Many subsequent changes in northern painting consist of the adaptation of Italian compositional realism to northern purposes.

ITALIAN GOTHIC PAINTERS

Giotto di Bondone was the most important Italian painter of the 14th century. Trained in Rome, Giotto executed his first important surviving work for the papal financier Enrico Scrovegni at the latter's family palace in Padua. The palace chapel, called the Arena Chapel (decorated *c.* 1305–13), is a masterpiece in which all the lessons of Roman mural painting were translated into a narrative sequence of great economy and expressiveness. In spite of the apparent realism of Giotto's work, however, the Byzantine past makes itself felt in the extremely strong sense of pattern and design noticeable throughout the compositions.

In Tuscany somewhat similar developments took place. Duccio's altarpiece, the "Maestà," contains a large number of small narrative scenes reminiscent of Giotto's frescoes. The figures, which have firmly modeled faces and expressive gestures, are arranged in buildings or landscapes that convincingly enclose them. Duccio's interest in realistic space, however, was much weaker than Giotto's. Although Duccio's scenes feature a

(continued on the next page)

(continued from the previous page)

variety of action and wealth of detail that, on the whole, is lacking in Giotto's early work, they do not make the same simple but dramatic impact. These conflicts are inherent in all realistic painting. In Giotto's work a shift in the balance between the two conflicting elements takes place.

Subsequent Florentine and Sienese painters also moved in this direction. Of the Sienese, Simone Martini was probably the most famous. His painting has strong suggestions of northern influence in its elegance and grace, but his care over detail is reminiscent of Duccio, and the careful structure of his setting recalls Giotto and the Roman painters. His major surviving work is now in Siena and Assisi, but some impressive remains have been recovered at Avignon.

Among other Tuscan painters were the brothers Pietro and Ambrogio Lorenzetti. Their major works are in Siena, but, again, there are important frescoes at Assisi. Ambrogio Lorenzetti is especially famous for an enormous landscape, illustrating the effect of good government, painted in the Palazzo Pubblico Siena (1338–39). Historically, it is the first large, realistic landscape in which Byzantine conventions were entirely discarded.

INTERNATIONAL GOTHIC

The style of European painting prevalent during the last half of the 14th century and the early years of the 15th is frequently called International Gothic. There were certainly at that time features common to European painting generally. In particular, figures were elegant and graceful, yet at the same time there was a certain artificiality about such figures, and a taste grew for realism in detail, general setting, and composition. The degree of internationalism about this phase of Gothic painting owes something to the fact that much of the most important work was executed under court patronage, and most European royal families were closely linked by marriage ties. Local idiosyncracies, however, persisted.

The main European courts were those of the Holy Roman emperors (who had nominal suzerainty over central Europe and who at this time had their capital at Prague), the Visconti of Milan, the Valois of France, and the Plantagenets of England. But other sources of patronage existed, and an extraordinary number of important painters were associated about 1350–1400 with the linguistic area of Low Germany—the Low Countries and Westphalia especially—and the Rhineland.

LATE GOTHIC

The key to much 15th-century painting in northern Europe lies in the Low Countries. The former influence of Paris and Dijon decreased, partly because of the renewal of the Hundred Years' War between England and France and partly because of the removal of the Burgundian court, after the mid-1420s, from Dijon to Brussels, which subsequently became the centre of an extensive court patronage.

The founder of the Flemish school of painting seems to have been Robert Campin of Tournai. The works of Campin, his pupil Rogier van der Weyden, and Jan van Eyck remained influential for the whole century. One of the most important discoveries of the period of about 1430 was the multifarious effects a painter can achieve by observing the action of light. These early Flemish artists found that light can define form, shape, and texture and that, when captured in a landscape, it can help convey a mood. Portraiture made dramatic progress during this period. Portraits were obviously not new, but the brilliant use of lighting gives the portraits of Jan van Eyck, for instance, a vivid life hitherto quite unknown. A great deal of later 15th- and 16th-century Flemish painting seems to play variations on these themes.

The influence of van Eyck's paintings was felt to a limited extent outside the Low

Countries. In the course of the century, however, the style of Rogier van der Weyden and his immediate successors became more influential, being felt in Germany, England, Spain, and Portugal. Any individualists at this time were usually painters who chose to go to the extreme of emphasizing the bizarre or the horrifying. Hugo van der Goes veered in this direction. Much more disquieting is the painting of Hiëronymus Bosch, whose strange scenes still puzzle and perplex. The work of Matthias Grünewald is grotesque and horrifying.

Rather different were the French painters of the 15th century. Court art revived, especially during the reign of Louis XI (1461–83), as exemplified by the illuminated manuscript *Le Livre du coeur d'amours éspris* (1465). The restrained and somewhat reticent character of much French painting is interestingly similar to much of the sculpture.

CHAPTER FOUR

PAINTING OF THE RENAISSANCE

The term "Renaissance" was first used by French art historians of the late 18th century in reference to the reappearance of antique architectural forms on Italian buildings of the early 16th century. The term was later expanded to include the whole of the 15th and 16th centuries and, by extension, to include sculpture, painting, and the decorative arts. Here the term is treated as a phenomenon that had its origins in Italy and then spread throughout western Europe.

The time span of the Renaissance is generally accepted as the period from roughly 1400 to about 1600, although certain geographical areas and certain art forms require greater latitude. This period is characterized as a rebirth or, better, the birth of attitudes and aims that have their closest parallel in the art of classical antiquity. The theoretical writings on art from the period indicate that man was the dominant theme. In religious painting, drama and emotion are expressed in human terms. This strongly humanistic trend serves to explain the development of portraiture as an independent genre and the ever-increasing number of profane, usually classical mythological, subjects in the art of the Renaissance. The painting of landscapes, as the earthly setting of man's activity, has its first modest beginnings in this period.

The role of art and of the artist began to take on modern form during the Renaissance. Leon Battista Alberti's *De pictura* (*Della pittura*), a treatise on the theory of painting, as opposed to the techniques of preparing and applying colours, appeared in Florence in 1435–36. The directions that art and art theory were to follow for the next 470 years are already present in this little book. The artist is considered to be a creator rather than a technician because he uses his intellect to measure, arrange, and harmonize the elements of his creation. The intellectual activity of art is demonstrated, by a series of comparisons, to be equivalent to that of the other liberal arts. Influences such as Alberti's book led to a new evaluation of the artist, with painters and their works being sought after by the rulers of Europe; the result was that great collections containing the works of major and minor masters were formed. At the same time the artist slowly began to free himself from the old guild system and to band together with his

HUMANISM

"Humanism" is a term that encompasses a variety of beliefs, methods, and philosophies that place central emphasis on the human realm. The term is most frequently used with reference to a system of education and mode of inquiry that developed in northern Italy during the 13th and 14th centuries and later spread through continental Europe and England. Known as "Renaissance humanism," this program was so broadly and profoundly influential that it is one of the chief reasons why the Renaissance is viewed as a distinct historical period. Indeed, though the word "Renaissance" is of more recent coinage, the fundamental idea of that period as one of renewal and reawakening is humanistic in origin. But humanism sought its own philosophical bases in far earlier times and, moreover, continued to exert some of its power long after the end of the Renaissance. Among the key principles and attitudes of humanism were classicism, realism, critical scrutiny and concern with detail, the emergence of the individual, the idea of the dignity of man, and an emphasis on virtuous actions.

colleagues, first in religious confraternities and later in academies of art, which, in turn, were to lead to the modern art school. During the Renaissance, practitioners of all the arts evolved from anonymous craftsmen to individuals, often highly respected ones. Painting became more intellectual, sometimes to its own disadvantage, and changed from serving as a vehicle for didacticism or decoration to becoming a self-aware, self-assured form of expression.

For the sake of convenience, painting of the Renaissance is divided into three periods. The early Renaissance is reckoned to cover the period from about 1420 to 1495. The High Renaissance, or classic phase, is generally considered to extend from 1495 to 1520 (the death of Raphael). The period of Mannerism and what has more recently been called late Renaissance painting is considered to extend from the 1520s to approximately 1600.

EARLY RENAISSANCE IN ITALY

The early Renaissance in Italy was essentially an experimental period characterized by the styles of individual artists rather than by any all-encompassing stylistic trend. Early Renaissance painting in Italy had its birth and development in Florence, from which it spread to other centres after the middle of the century.

The political and economic climate of the Italian Renaissance was often unstable; Florence, however, did at least provide an intellectual and cultural environment that was extremely favorable for the development of art. Although the direct impact of humanist literary studies upon 15th-century painting has generally been denied, three writers of the 15th century (Alberti, Filarete, and Enea Silvio Piccolomini, later Pope Pius II) drew parallels between the rebirth of classical learning and the rebirth of art. The literature of antiquity revealed that in earlier times both works of art and artists had been appreciated for their own intrinsic merits. Humanist studies also fostered a tendency to see the world and everything in it in human terms. In the early 15th century, Masaccio emphasized the human drama and emotions in his painting *The Expulsion* rather than the theological implications of the act portrayed. Masaccio and his contemporaries seem to be more concerned with the human relations between the figures in their compositions than with the purely devotional aspects of the subject.

In the same way, painters became more and more concerned with the relations between the work of art and the observer. This latter aspect of early 15th-century Florentine painting relies in great part on the invention of the one-point perspective system, which derives in turn from the new learning and the new vision of the world. In this system all parts of the painting bear a rational relation to each other and to the observer, for the observer's height and the distance he is to stand from the painting are controlled by the artist in laying out his perspective construction. By means of this system the microcosm of the painting and the real world of the observer become visually one, and the observer participates, as it were, in what he observes.

To heighten the illusion of a painting as a window on the world, the Italian artists of the early 15th century turned to a study of the effects of light in nature and how to represent them in a painting, a study of the anatomy and proportions of man, and a careful observation of the world about them. It is primarily these characteristics that separate early Renaissance painting from late medieval painting in Italy.

MASACCIO

Masaccio has rightly been called the father of Renaissance painting, for every major artist of the 15th and 16th centuries in Florence began his career by studying Masaccio's murals in fresco. Masaccio's extant work reveals a concern with large and simple figures clad in simple draperies. He was concerned with light and the way it gives the illusion of solidity to the painted figure. He created a deep and clearly articulated space in his paintings, and he was above all concerned with his actors as humans carrying out some purposeful human activity.

The only extant work by Masaccio that can be clearly dated is the Pisa altarpiece of 1426, the central panel of which depicts the Madonna enthroned with Christ Child and angels. Although Masaccio continued the medieval tradition of using a gold background, the architectural elements of the throne indicate his awareness of the influence of Roman antiquity on the architecture of his contemporary and friend Filippo Brunelleschi. The Madonna is no longer an elegant queen of heaven but an earthly mother with a human child on her lap. The figure of the Christ Child is a clear demonstration for future generations of the way light and shade can be manipulated in a painting to give the illusion of a solid three-dimensional body.

Masaccio's great fresco series in the Brancacci Chapel of Santa Maria del Carmine in Florence adds yet another dimension to early Renaissance painting. In this narrative sequence devoted to the life of St. Peter, he chose the most important moment in the narrative and then emphasized the drama by the human reactions to it. In this same chapel Masaccio also demonstrated his awareness of the real world, for the light of the paintings, indicated by the cast shadows, is the same as the natural light falling into the chapel.

The Tribute Money, fresco by Masaccio, 1425; in the Brancacci Chapel, Santa Maria del Carmine, Florence

The Trinity in Santa Maria Novella, Florence, provides a summary of Masaccio's brief career and indeed of the aesthetic principles of early Renaissance painting generally. In addition to the use of light to unite the space of the painting with the space of the observer, Masaccio also employed what appears to be the earliest practical example of the one-point perspective system, later to be formulated in words by Alberti. All the highest aims of early Renaissance painting are here: simplicity, strength, monumentality;

man as observer, as actor, and as participant in the work of art.

FLORENTINE PAINTERS OF THE MID-15TH CENTURY

Masaccio had no true followers or successors of equal stature, though there was a group of other Florentine painters who were about the same age as Masaccio and who followed in his footsteps to a greater or lesser degree: Fra Filippo Lippi, Fra Angelico, and Paolo Uccello.

Fra Filippo Lippi was a Carmelite monk who spent his youth and early manhood at Santa Maria del Carmine, where Masaccio's work was daily before his eyes. Lippi's work further developed the characteristics of Masaccio's painting of human figures. His style would also become a key source for later Renaissance portraiture, including Leonardo da Vinci's *Mona Lisa*, and a direct inspiration for the work of his student, Botticelli.

Born about the same time as Masaccio, Fra Angelico's earliest documented work continues much that is traditional to medieval art, although it already reveals the influence of Masaccio. The altarpiece that he executed between 1438 and 1440 for the high altar of San Marco is one of the landmarks of early Renaissance art. It is the first appearance in Florence of the *sacra conversazione*, a composition in which angels, saints, and sometimes donors occupy the same space as the Madonna and Christ Child and in which the figures seem to be engaged in conversation. In addition to inaugurating a new phase of religious painting, the altarpiece reveals the influence of Masaccio in the sculptural treatment of the figures and an accurate awareness of the perspective theories of painting expressed by Alberti in his treatise.

Paolo Uccello's reputation as a practitioner of perspective is such that his truly remarkable gifts as a decorator tend to be overlooked. Studies of his extant works suggest that he was more interested in medieval optics than in the rational perspective system of Alberti and Brunelleschi. Uccello is perhaps best known for the three panels depicting *The Battle of San Romano*, executed about 1456 for the Medici Palace. The paintings were designed as wall decoration and as such resemble tapestries: Uccello is concerned only with creating a small boxlike space for the action, closing off the background with a tapestry-like interweaving of men and animals. His primary concern is with the rhythmic disposition of the elements of the composition across the surface, an emphasis that he reinforces with the repetition of arcs and circles.

Masaccio's greatest impact can be seen in the works of three younger painters, Andrea del Castagno, Domenico Veneziano, and Piero della Francesca. Castagno was the leader of the group. His *Last Supper* of about 1445, in the former convent of Sant'Apollonia in Florence, reveals the influence of Masaccio in the sculptural treatment of the figures, the painter's concern with light, and his desire to create a credible and rationally conceived space. At the same time Castagno betrays an almost pedantic interest in antiquity by the use of fictive marble panels on the rear wall and of sphinxes for the bench ends, both of which are direct copies of Roman prototypes. In the last years of his life, Castagno's style changed abruptly; he adopted a highly expressive emotionalism that paralleled a similar development in the work of his contemporaries. The optimism, rationality, and calm human drama of earlier Renaissance painting in Florence were beginning to give way to a more personal, expressive, and linear style.

One aspect of this new direction is met in the work of the enigmatic Domenico Veneziano, the second of the three principal painters who looked to Masaccio. He was from Venice and arrived in Florence about 1438. His St. Lucy altarpiece of about 1445–50 is an example of the *sacra conversazione* genre and contains references to the painting of Masaccio. The colour, however, is Domenico's own and has no relation to the Florentine tradition. His juxtaposition of pinks and light greens and his generally blond tonality point rather to his

Venetian origins. In the painting he has lowered the vanishing point in order to make the figures appear to tower over the observer, with the result that the monumentality of the painting is enhanced at the expense of the observer's sense of participating in the painting.

Piero della Francesca received his early training in Florence but spent the active part of his career outside the city in other centres. His *Flagellation of Christ* (late 1450s) is a summary of early 15th-century interest in mathematics, perspective, and proportion. The calm sculptural figures are placed in clear, rational space and bathed in a cool light. This gives them a monumental dignity that can only be compared to early 5th-century-BCE Greek sculpture.

LATE 15TH-CENTURY FLORENTINE PAINTERS

A hiatus occurred in Florentine painting around 1465–75. All the older artists had died, and the men who were to dominate the second half of the century were too young to have had prolonged contact with them. Three of these younger artists, Antonio Pollaiuolo, Sandro Botticelli, and Andrea del Verrocchio, began their careers as goldsmiths, which perhaps explains the linear emphasis and sense of movement noticeable in Florentine painting of the later 15th century.

As well as being a goldsmith, Pollaiuolo was a painter, sculptor, engraver, and architect. His work indicates his fascination with muscles in action, and he is said to have been the first artist to dissect the human body. In the altarpiece *The Martyrdom of St. Sebastian* (1475) he presents the archers from two points of view to demonstrate their muscular activity. His painting and small sculpture *Hercules and Antaeus,* like the engraving *The Battle of the Nudes,* depict struggle and violent action. *The Rape of Deianira* emphasizes yet another new element in Florentine painting, the landscape setting, in this case a lovely portrait of the Arno Valley with the city of Florence in the background.

A similar concern with moving figures, a sense of movement across the surface of the panel, and landscape is found in the earlier works of Sandro Botticelli. In his well-known painting *The Primavera* he uses line in depicting hair, flowing draperies, or the contour of an arm to suggest the movement of the figures. At the same time the pose and gesture of the figures set up a rising and falling linear movement across the surface of the painting. Botticelli's well-known paintings of the Madonna and Child reveal a sweetness that he may have learned from Fra Filippo Lippi, together with his own sense of elegance and grace. A certain nervosity and pessimistic introspection inherent in Botticelli's early works broke forth about 1490. His *Mystic Nativity* of

1501 is even, in one sense, a denial of all that the Renaissance stood for. The ambiguities of space and proportion are directed toward the unprecedented creation of a highly personal and emotionally charged statement.

Florentine painters active in the closing decades of the 15th century include Andrea del Verrocchio, who is best known as the master of Leonardo da Vinci and Perugino.

Sandro Botticelli's painting *Primavera* ("Springtime") presents the pregnant figure of Spring in the center. The god Mercury and the three Graces are on the left. On the right are Flora, goddess of flowering plants, and a nymph pursued by the North Wind.

There was also Filippino Lippi, who was apparently apprenticed to Botticelli when his father, Fra Filippo Lippi, died; he painted a group of Madonnas that are easily confused with Botticelli's early work. By 1485, however, he had developed a somewhat nervous and agitated style that can be seen in the highly expressive *Vision of St. Bernard* in the Badia, Florence. His last works, such as the series of frescoes he painted in Santa Maria Novella (1502), reveal a use of colour and distortion of form that may have influenced the later development of Mannerism in Florence a generation or so later. Another painter active at this time was Domenico Ghirlandajo, whose artistic career was spent as a reporter of the Florentine scene. The series of frescoes on the *Life of the Virgin* in Santa Maria Novella (finished 1490) can be viewed as the life of a young Florentine girl as well as a religious painting. His art was already old-fashioned in his own time, but he provided a large number of Florentine artists, among them Michelangelo, with training in the difficult art of fresco painting.

DIFFUSION OF THE INNOVATIONS OF THE FLORENTINE SCHOOL

The discoveries and innovations of the early 15th century in Florence began to diffuse to other artistic centres by mid-century. Siena painters in general continued the traditions of the 14th century. In Ferrara, the influence of Florence was felt as transmitted by Piero della Francesca. Only in Padua and Venice, however, did painters arise who could actually challenge the preeminence of Florence.

Andrea Mantegna was influenced by the sculpture executed by Donatello in Padua, the art of antiquity around him, and the teaching of his master, Francesco Squarcione. The frescoes he completed in 1455 in the Ovetari Chapel of the Eremitani Church in Padua grew out of the traditions of Florence, traditions to which Mantegna gave his own special stamp, however. His space is like that devised by the Florentines except that he lowers the horizon line to give his figures greater monumentality. His sculptural and often stony figures descend from Donatello and from ancient Roman models. His use of decorative details from antiquity reveals the almost archaeological training that he had received from Squarcione. By 1460 Mantegna had moved to Mantua. His altarpieces, interpretation of antiquity, and engravings made him preeminent in northern Italy and a strong influence on his contemporaries and successors.

The Bellini family of Venice forms one of the great dynasties in painting. The father, Jacopo, who had been a student of Gentile da Fabriano, adopted a style that owed something to both that prevailing in the Low

Countries and that in Italy; he also compiled an important sketchbook. A daughter of Jacopo's was married to Mantegna, and the two sons—Gentile and Giovanni Bellini—dominated Venetian painting until the first decade of the 16th century. Gentile followed more closely in his father's footsteps. Giovanni early fell under the influence of Mantegna. However the two were stylistically close and both relied on Jacopo Bellini's sketchbook. At an unknown point in his career, Giovanni was in addition introduced to Flemish painting. These different influences permitted him about 1480 to evolve a highly personal style that greatly influenced the work of subsequent Venetian painters, including Lorenzo Lotto and Vittore Carpaccio and also, more importantly, Giorgione and Titian.

LEONARDO DA VINCI

The richness and the variety of 15th-century Florentine painting are both embodied and transformed in the art and the person of the multifaceted genius Leonardo da Vinci. Although he devoted a great deal of his career to a theoretical treatise on the art of painting, he was above all interested in the appearance of things and in the way they operated. His consummate skill as a draftsman made it possible for him to record his discoveries as no man before him had done. All the knowledge that he gained was directed toward enriching his art, for Leonardo thought of himself primarily as a painter.

As a youth Leonardo was apprenticed to Verrocchio, in whose shop he learned to draw, prepare and mix colours, and paint. He probably also learned how to model in wax and clay and how to cast bronze, as well as the art of sculpting in marble. Leonardo's genius is already apparent in his collaboration with Verrocchio in the *Baptism of Christ* (*c.* 1474–75), in which his contributions to the landscape and his figure of an angel clearly reveal his superiority. In the painting, he makes a synthesis of the divergent tendencies of the compositions of the first half of the century and creates a composition that is at once ordered and free, calm and full of movement, simple and varied. The nature of this composition and the preparatory underpainting of the figures and landscapes clearly demonstrate that Leonardo had advanced far beyond his contemporaries.

In 1481 Leonardo offered his services to the Duke of Milan, and for the following 18 years he remained in Milan. *The Virgin of the Rocks*, painted in Milan about 1483, stands at the threshold of the High Renaissance. In this painting Leonardo introduced the pyramidal composition that was to become a hallmark of the period. The placement of the Madonna, the Christ Child, the young St. John the Baptist, and the angel creates a movement that the eye willingly follows, yet the movement is contained within the implied pyramid, giving a sense of stability and calm grandeur to the composition. The mysterious landscape that surrounds them implies adequate space in which the figures can exist and move and an extension into depth that the eye cannot follow. The light that falls on the figures delicately models them in a subtle juxtaposition of light and shade. The contours of the figures seem to dissolve into the background, and the light seems to flow gently over a surface. The subtle and delicate modeling and the suggestive smoky atmosphere are known as sfumato. More important and influential was Leonardo's use of light and shade as a unifying compositional factor. This was unprecedented in painting. It was achieved by the tonal continuity of the shadows—a tonal continuity conditional upon a severe restriction of local colour.

These effects, as well as the softly diffused light characteristic of Venetian painting, were only possible in the oil medium, which, because of its lengthy drying period, enables all parts of a painting to be advanced and adjusted together and the transparent glazes of which make possible unity of atmosphere and chiaroscuro. The rich effects of impasto (deliberately rough and thick paint textures) were also made possible in oil and were particularly exploited in Venice, where the use of canvas as a support

SFUMATO

Derived from the Italian word *sfumare*, "to tone down" or "to evaporate like smoke," sfumato is the fine shading in painting or drawing that produces soft, imperceptible transitions between colours and tones. The term is used most often in connection with the work of Leonardo da Vinci and his followers, who made subtle gradations, without lines or borders, from light to dark areas. The technique was used for a highly illusionistic rendering of facial features and for atmospheric effects.

first became truly popular. But there is no doubt that oil painting is a technique that originated in the Low Countries.

Leonardo's attempts to transfer this new concept of painting to the difficult genre of murals led to the triumph and the tragedy of *The Last Supper* (1495–98). Because the traditional technique of fresco painting was too final for Leonardo's method of working, he invented a new technique that permitted him to revise in the manner of oil painting. The technique was not permanent, and the painting began to deteriorate in Leonardo's own lifetime. Despite its deterioration the painting stands as one of man's greatest achievements. All elements of the painting lead the eye to the calm and pyramidal figure of Christ. The room is depicted according to the rules of perspective, with all the direction implied by the lines of the architecture meeting at the vanishing point in the head of Christ. In this painting Leonardo has combined the sense of drama of the groups

of disturbed apostles, the sculptural figure of Christ, and the rationally constructed space of the first half of the 15th century with the movement and emotion of the second half, achieving a new synthesis that goes far beyond anything his predecessors had dreamed was possible. Leonardo's *The Last Supper* marks the actual beginning of the High Renaissance in Italy.

The Last Supper, fresco by Leonardo da Vinci, 1495–98; in Santa Maria delle Grazie, Milan

HIGH RENAISSANCE IN ITALY

In painting, the style called High Renaissance or classic is, in a sense, the culmination of the experiments of the 15th century, for it is above all characterized by a desire to achieve harmony and balance. Movement is important and necessary, yet the eye is always given a point of focus and rest. The composition is self-contained. Although there is movement implied in the poses of the figures and movement across the surface of the composition, it is always dignified movement, giving the impression of calm. The style exhibits variety and richness, yet maintains simplicity and unity. It is never as self-conscious as 15th-century painting had been, nor is it as laboured as much of Mannerist painting. It is frequently compared to Greek art of the 5th century BCE. Its greatest practitioners were the Florentines Leonardo da Vinci and Michelangelo, the Urbino-born Raphael, and the Venetian Titian. Other lesser artists were attracted to the style at varying point in their careers.

LEONARDO, RAPHAEL, AND MICHELANGELO

The new style of painting that Leonardo had invented in Milan was continued with modifications by Bernardino Luini and others.

However it had no immediate repercussions in his native Florence. The full impact of Leonardo's art was felt only upon his return to Florence in 1500. Crowds flocked to the church of the Santissima Annunziata to see his cartoon of *The Virgin and Child with St. Anne.* Leonardo's great mural of the *Battle of Anghiari* (1503–06) pitted him against his rival Michelangelo in a competition to record the history of the city in the seat of city government. Neither painting was finished. Yet, despite the inconclusive nature of the works partially executed during his brief Florentine stay, Leonardo left a deep impression on that city. The *Mona Lisa* revolutionized portrait painting. Leonardo's drawings encouraged fellow artists to make more and freer studies for their paintings and encouraged connoisseurs to collect those

Mona Lisa, oil on wood panel by Leonardo da Vinci, *c.* 1503–06; in the Louvre, Paris

drawings. Through the drawings his Milanese works were made known to the Florentines. Finally, his reputation and stature as an artist and thinker spread to his fellow artists and assured for them a freedom of action and thought similar to his own.

The painter who benefited most from the example of Leonardo was undoubtedly Raphael. Born Raphael Sanzio, he was as a youth under the influence of Perugino. He was already a successful and respected artist when, at age 21, he came to Florence only to discover that all he had learned and practiced was old-fashioned and provincial. He immediately set about learning from the Florentines. His drawing style changed from the tight contours and interior hatching he had learned from Perugino toward the freer, more flowing style of Leonardo. From Leonardo's *Virgin of the Rocks* he evolved a new Madonna type seated in a soft and gentle landscape. He adopted the *Mona Lisa* format for his portraits, and he also studied closely the sculpture of Michelangelo. By 1509, when he departed for Rome, Raphael had assimilated all Florence had to offer and was ready to make his own unique statement.

The Stanza della Segnatura (the first of a series of rooms in the Vatican papal apartments), particularly the *School of Athens*, which Raphael painted between 1508 and 1511, is one of the clearest and finest examples of the High Renaissance style. In the *School of Athens* Raphael, like Leonardo before him, made a balance between the movement of the figures and the ordered and stable space. He peopled this space with figures in a rich variety of controlled poses and gestures to make one group lead to the next in an interweaving and interlocking pattern, bringing the eye to the central figures of Plato and Aristotle at the converging point of the perspective construction. The unity, variety, and harmony of High Renaissance felicitously combine in the frescoes that decorate the Stanza della Segnatura.

At about the same time Raphael was working in the papal apartments in the Vatican, Michelangelo had undertaken the formidable task of decorating the ceiling of the Sistine Chapel (1508–12), also for Pope Julius II. In 1481–82 under Pope Sixtus IV, the chapel had been completed and the walls decorated with frescoes depicting scenes from the life of Moses and the life of Christ executed by Botticelli, Ghirlandajo, Perugino, and others. Against his will Michelangelo was assigned to paint in fresco scenes from the creation. Although he had been trained in fresco painting in the shop of Ghirlandajo and although he had already executed a few paintings of considerable power, Michelangelo thought of himself as a sculptor. He engaged a group of his former colleagues and with them began to paint the *Drunkenness of Noah* above the entrance to the chapel. Michelangelo had little patience with his less gifted associates, dismissed them, and executed the entire ceiling alone. The scenes were painted in reverse chronological order, beginning with the *Drunkenness of Noah* over the door and ending with the act of creation over the altar. In the progressive frescoes Michelangelo stylistically moves beyond his contemporaries to a highly personal statement without parallel in the art of the 16th century. The Sistine ceiling was recognized as a masterpiece in its own time. The artist was judged to be a superhuman being and earned the title "the divine Michelangelo."

Michelangelo, Leonardo, and Raphael raised the artist and his art to a position of esteem perhaps never enjoyed either before or since. Certainly their soaring levels of achievement made it difficult for succeeding artists to follow in their footsteps and impossible to surpass them. Hence, the "anticlassic style," as it has been called, emerged in their own

lifetime—even in some of Raphael's late works—
and provided one of the sources of Mannerism.
By 1513, when Julius II died and Leo X
was elected pope, the three great painters

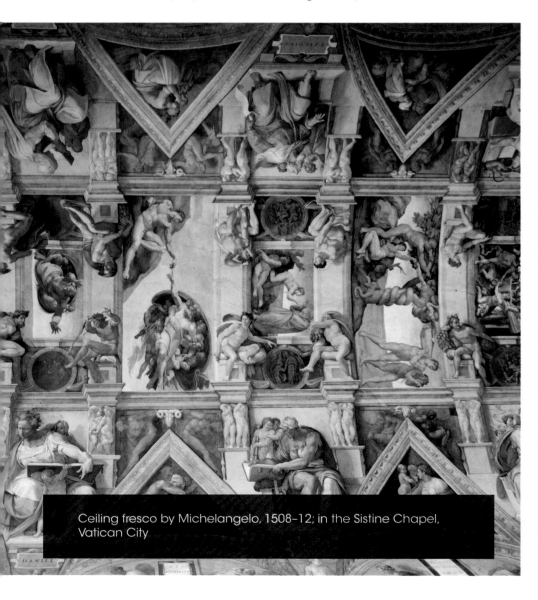

Ceiling fresco by Michelangelo, 1508–12; in the Sistine Chapel,
Vatican City.

of the High Renaissance became involved in projects that diverted them from the paths they had hitherto been following. Nevertheless the ideals of the High Renaissance as they appeared in the works of Leonardo, Raphael, and Michelangelo continued to develop independently in areas outside Rome and Florence. Most notably, in Parma the painter Antonio Allegri, better known as Correggio, formed his art under the influence of Mantegna and Leonardo's Milanese followers. Correggio is perhaps best known for his frescoes at Parma in the cathedral and in the church of San Giovanni Evangelista, which seem to prefigure the style of painting found in the Baroque.

THE HIGH RENAISSANCE IN VENICE

In the late 15th century, painting in Venice traveled much the same paths toward the High Renaissance as in Florence, while still maintaining a purely Venetian flavour. Giovanni Bellini's Madonnas of 1505–10 are stylistically similar to the Madonnas that Raphael was painting in Florence at about the same time. The San Zaccaria altarpiece (*Enthroned Madonna with Four Saints*) of 1505 carries the *sacra conversazione* fully into the High Renaissance. Inasmuch as Giovanni Bellini dominated Venetian painting, his style influenced the younger painters Giorgione and Titian, yet he was receptive enough to learn in turn from them and inventive enough to maintain his position of dominance.

Giorgione, having learned from Bellini, went beyond his master to bring to Venetian painting a treatment of landscape that can only be compared to pastoral poetry. In his brief career this highly inventive young artist taught his contemporaries and successors how to exploit the medium of oil paint to create the illusion of textures, light, and air in their paintings. Through his works Giorgione reveals the Venetians' predisposition toward textures, carefully rendering almost palpable the appearance of flesh, fabric, wood, stone, and foliage. His use of landscape to create a mood and the use of figures in the landscape to reflect or intensify that mood is an innovation characteristic of Venetian painting of the 16th century and one of great importance to the development of Baroque art. Landscape painting was to become a specialization of artists only toward the close of the 16th century, and even then chiefly in northern Europe.

The impact of Giorgione on Venetian art was immediate and direct. Giorgione's greatest impact was on Titian (Tiziano Vecelli). Although Titian was never a student of Giorgione, he worked with him on one project and finished a number of his paintings. The influence of Giorgione is especially marked in the profane paintings just as the religious paintings are marked by the influence of Bellini, Titian's teacher and rival until his death, when Titian himself emerged as the leader of Venetian painting.

Titian's great masterpiece, the *Assumption* (1516–18), established his reputation as Bellini's successor. In the painting he exhibits the Venetians' love of colour and texture, but he succeeds in achieving a balanced and moving composition that can only be compared to Raphael's work in its grandeur. The environment is both earth and heaven, yet it is created and defined by light and atmosphere in a typically Venetian way, rather than by architecture, as would have been more common in Florence.

Upon the completion of the *Assumption* Titian undertook to execute a series of paintings on mythological themes for the court of Ferrara. In *The Bacchanal* Titian reveals his mastery in treating mythological subjects. The bacchants are disposed about the miraculous stream of wine that flows through an island, dancing, singing, and drinking. The movement of the figures, the juxtaposition of nude and clothed, of male and female, creates a revel in which even the landscape seems to participate—only a Venetian could have created such a pagan, earthy, and hedonistic glorification of life.

On a trip to Rome in 1545 Titian succeeded in rivaling the works of Raphael and Michelangelo, while demonstrating that Venetian painting in its own unique way was the equal of the Florentine-Roman tradition. In his late works Titian carried the oil medium to new heights. He used loosely juxtaposed patches of colour, sometimes allowing the prepared canvas to show through. He applied paint freely and loosely with the brush and sometimes reworked it with his fingers. Although his paintings have a fresh quality that makes them appear to have been painted quickly in the heat of inspiration, it is known from his biographers and friends that each work had been carefully studied, criticized, and reworked before the artist was satisfied.

Titian's genius, given full rein in his long and productive career, deeply influenced Venetian painting. The two most outstanding painters of the end of the 16th century, Veronese and Tintoretto, each took a different aspect of Titian's style and developed it. Paolo Caliari, called Veronese (he was born in Verona), is best known for the rich colour and interweaving compositions he learned from Titian. With Tintoretto he decorated the chambers of the Doges' Palace in Venice, partially supplanting the aging and busy Titian as official painter of the city. Jacopo Robusti, called Tintoretto, was most interested in Titian's use of dramatic light and heightened emotion. By 1548 he had established his reputation as a leading artist of the younger generation with his *San Marco Freeing the Slave*. He decorated several chambers of the Doges' Palace with a number of inventive mythological scenes. A great part of his career and energy was devoted to the decoration of the Great School of San Rocco, Venice (1564–*c*. 1588). Perhaps the crowning achievement of his career can be found in *The Last Supper* of 1594, painted for the church of San Giorgio Maggiore, Venice. In this painting Tintoretto made use of all the rapidly receding diagonals and dramatic foreshortenings of the Mannerist vocabulary, but he brought to

The Last Supper, oil on canvas by Tintoretto, 1594; in the church of San Giorgio Maggiore, Venice.

the painting the Venetians' use of light effects to define the forms and heighten the drama.

With the death of Titian, Tintoretto, and Veronese, Venice became a school for 17th-century painters, where great works of the past were studied but few great works were produced until the 18th century.

ITALIAN MANNERISM AND LATE RENAISSANCE

The first reaction against Leonardo, Michelangelo, and Raphael occurred in Florence between 1515 and 1524, during which time the painters Giovanni Battista (called Rosso Fiorentino) and Jacopo Carrucci Pontormo decisively broke away from the harmony and naturalism of the High Renaissance style. Their movement, particularly what might be called their aesthetic anarchy, attracted the sympathetic attention of some 20th-century art historians, largely because of affinities such art historians saw between their work and modern trends, particularly Expressionism. German art historian Max Dvořák called these 16th-century nonconformists Mannerists. Later historians suggested, however, that the term "Mannerism" could more accurately be applied to a very different style initiated in Rome about 1520.

Roman Mannerism, which subsequently spread throughout Europe, is characterized by a display of the artificiality of art, a thoroughly self-conscious cultivation of elegance and facility, and a sophisticated delight in the bizarre.

The term "Mannerism" is ultimately derived from the Italian word *maniera* (literally "style"). It was in the 16th century that *maniera* was first consistently used in art criticism to indicate a definable quality—that of stylishness. Artist biographer Giorgio Vasari attributed this absolute quality of stylishness to Leonardo, Michelangelo, and Raphael, and, above all, to artists of his own day who had learned their styles from studying these great masters. Standing at the head of the enormous representational discoveries of the Renaissance and with an increased knowledge of antiquity, Vasari was convinced that his contemporaries were in a position to understand the secret of true artistic style. This was the *maniera*.

Taking Vasari's quality of *maniera* as the key to Mannerism, it is possible to outline some of its hallmarks. In figure style, the standard of formal complexity had been set by Michelangelo and that of idealized beauty by Raphael. In the art of their followers, obsession with style in figure composition often outweighed the importance of the subject matter. The highest value was placed upon the apparently effortless solution of considerable artistic problems, such as the portrayal of the nude figure in complex poses.

While depending heavily upon ancient Roman art for many of its decorative motifs and standards of design, Mannerist style commonly exploited a certain degree of license within the classical vocabulary—what Vasari and contemporary literary theorists called "a departure from the normal usage."

It was in the intellectualizing atmosphere of the Italian courts that Mannerism met with the greatest favour. There the conscious intricacies of Mannerist compositions and the eloquent quotations from antiquity were appreciated. Mannerism was first and foremost a connoisseur's art—certainly not one that appealed to a churchman. It is not surprising that the later Mannerist painters were censured by the church during the Counter-Reformation for painting altarpieces that were intended to demonstrate the virtuosity of their creators rather than illustrate a religious story. These factors caused the style to fall into general disrepute.

THE RENAISSANCE OUTSIDE ITALY

The early and High Renaissance style as developed in Italy did not immediately dominate all European painting. A few northern artists adopted Renaissance motifs but used them in a piecemeal manner without full comprehension of Italian compositional methods. After 1520, however, northern and Spanish artists came increasingly to understand and adopt Mannerist ideas, and highly individual schools of Mannerism began to appear in various centres outside Italy. Regional styles of considerable decorative flamboyance resulted from the fusion of the intricacies of the late Gothic style with the complexities of Mannerism.

FRANCE

Francis I, king of France (1515–47), was enamoured with all things Italian. He commissioned and imported Italian artists to design, build, and decorate his palaces. Rosso Fiorentino arrived in France in 1530, followed two years later by his fellow Italian, the Mannerist Francesco Primaticcio. In the gallery of Francis I at Fontainebleau, Rosso initiated a new and intricate decorative system in which stucco and painting form a richly luxuriant complex—the plastic realization of the late Raphaelesque decorative manner. Primaticcio, who had been trained by Giulio Romano at Mantua and influenced by Parmigianino, took over Rosso's leading position on the latter's death in 1540. French artists at the court, such as the two Jean Cousins and Antoine Caron, quickly adopted aspects of Italian Mannerism to create a style of painting characterized as the school of Fontainebleau.

SPAIN

During the first decade of the 16th century, Fernando Yáñez, who may have assisted Leonardo da Vinci on the *Battle of Anghiari* in 1505, executed works showing a good knowledge of Italian Renaissance developments. Further Italianate tendencies emerged strongly in the Valencian works of Juan de Macip and his son Juan de Juanes. Full-fledged Mannerism made its appearance in the Seville cathedral in the *Descent from the Cross* (1547) by Pedro Campaña (Pieter de Kempeneer), an artist from Brussels, and subsequently in the refined court portraiture of Anthonis Mor (Sir Anthony More) and Alonso Sánchez Coello, whose royal portraits possess an elegance reminiscent of Bronzino's Florentine style. Although Campaña's paintings are Mannerist in composition, they also foreshadow the expressiveness characteristic of Spanish style in the hands of Luis de Morales and El Greco.

From 1546 until his death in 1586, Morales remained almost exclusively in the provincial isolation of Badajoz, developing a highly individual art of great spiritual intensity, radically separated from the Mannerist mainstream. El Greco, though born in Crete, was more fully conversant with Italian painting, having studied with Titian in Venice and later residing in Rome for two years. His Spanish paintings exploit the anatomical attenuations of Roman Mannerism, but the vividly emotional qualities of his colour and paint handling depend almost entirely upon Venetian precedents. Under the influence of Counter-Reformation mysticism in Toledo after 1575, he developed an increasingly personal and nonrealistic manner, indulging in space and supernatural light effects. The narrative fervour of his style stands in sharp contrast to the stylish formalism of international Mannerism.

GERMANY

Albrecht Dürer was the first important German artist who displayed a profound understanding of Italian Renaissance art and theory. In 1494 he made a brief trip to Italy, where he studied the works of Mantegna and the Venetians. In 1505–07 he was again in Italy and was on intimate terms with Giovanni Bellini. Dürer was interested in what he felt to be the "secrets" of Italian art and in the new humanism carried north by his peers. As a result, his paintings maintain the northerners' taste for detail, rendered meticulously in oil, but he joined to it the Italian interest in broadly conceived compositions.

Although he executed a large number of important paintings, Dürer is perhaps best known for his woodcuts and engravings, by which he raised printmaking from a minor to a major art.

In the 16th century the Renaissance, as far as German painting was concerned, tended to follow the lines established by Dürer. Two artists of note do emerge, but their styles are so individual that they do not represent a national school.

Lucas Cranach the Elder was deeply influenced by Dürer and the Danube school, an early 16th-century tradition of landscape painting that was in some ways a transition between the styles of Gothic and Renaissance painting. By 1505 he had moved to Wittenberg and become court painter to the electors of Saxony. There his style changed radically, epitomizing the dichotomy that existed in 16th-century northern European painting. He developed in Wittenberg the full-length portrait in which the sitter is rendered with consummate skill and fidelity. Cranach was a personal friend of Martin Luther and is probably best known for his portraits of the great reformer.

Hans Holbein the Younger was trained by his father in Augsburg but took up residence in Basel, Switzerland, about 1515. He early developed a portrait style that was greatly sought after by the burghers of Basel. In 1526 he made his first trip to London, and in 1532 religious troubles in Basel were so intense that he accepted a position at the English court and left the city forever. Holbein's portraits were all painted with a great understanding of the sitter and often have a note of Italian elegance. His surfaces tend to be tight and hard, yet there is a certain expansiveness created by the positioning within the frame. He established a portrait tradition in England and also contributed to the popularity of the miniature in that country.

LOW COUNTRIES

In the Low Countries there emerged early in the 16th century a group of painters misleadingly lumped together as the Antwerp Mannerists. Their exaggerated and fanciful compositions descend in great part from the decorative excesses of late Gothic art, generally with some Italianate details probably transmitted by architects' and goldsmiths' pattern books.

The Flemish painter Jan Gossaert visited Rome in 1508. At first he continued his ornate late Gothic style, but by 1514 he began to adopt the great innovations occurring in Italian painting. His mythological paintings indicate that he was able to understand only the superficialities and not the motivation and *terribilità* (awesome power) of Michelangelo's nudes. Bernard van Orley remained in Brussels and learned of Italy through Raphael's cartoons, which were sent to Brussels to be woven into tapestries. Before the end of the century, Dutch painters such as Jan van Scorel, Maerten van Heemskerck, and Sir Anthony More were absorbing Italian influences.

Pieter Bruegel the Elder visited Italy in 1551–53 but was more influenced by the country's landscape than by Italian painting. He was also a great observer of peasant life. His paintings illustrating Low Countries' proverbs and children's games reveal an interest in popular themes and common life rather than in the pedantic Romanizing compositions of some of his contemporaries. This subject matter, latent from the early 15th century in the Low Countries, was given new dimensions by Bruegel. His *Harvesters* (1565) displays a remarkable sensitivity to colour and pattern. The intense golden yellow of the ripe wheat sets up a bold pattern across the lower half of the picture and contrasts with the cool greens and blues of the limitless plain stretching off into the distance. Some figures move across a lane cut through the wheat, while others cut into what seems a solid space. The sleeping peasants resting after their noon meal are disposed in patterns and poses that make one feel the heat and calm of the summer's day. This sympathetic view of

Peasant Dance, oil on wood by Pieter Bruegel the Elder, *c.* 1568; in the Kunsthistorisches Museum, Vienna

peasant life, with its bold geometric patterns, runs throughout the series of the months and recurs in *The Wedding Dance* (1566) and *Peasant Dance* (c. 1568) and *Peasant Wedding* (c. 1567).

Bruegel brought to an end the 16th century in the north and prepared the way for the Baroque. His sons and grandsons were important painters who helped to train some of the leading artists of the 17th century in the Low

Countries. It was the elder Bruegel, however, who made landscape and peasant life an accepted subject for painting in the Renaissance.

The Mannerist style was not comprehended as soon in the 16th century in the Low Countries as it had been in France or Spain. With the notable exception of Frans Floris, it was not until the generation of artists born during the middle years of the century that Mannerism was fully assimilated. This generation of Flemish and Dutch Mannerists was influenced chiefly by the Italian Mannerists of the second half of the century.

BOHEMIA

By far the most ambitious patron of Mannerist art in Europe north of Italy was the Holy Roman emperor Rudolf II, who in the late 1570s established his court at Prague. Between the end of the 16th century and the beginning of the 17th, Rudolf employed architects, sculptors, and painters to create impressive artistic works for his court. Bartholomaeus Spranger's *Allegory of Rudolf II* indicates the quality of Rudolf's court art and its clear Mannerist sympathies—sensually graceful figures clad in the dress of classical antiquity and a cultivated facility in composition and execution.

CHAPTER FIVE

THE BAROQUE

The term "Baroque" is loosely applied to European art from the end of the 16th century to the early 18th century, the latter part of this period being generally designated as Late Baroque. The painting of the Baroque period is so varied that no single set of stylistic criteria can be applied to it. This is partly because the painting of Roman Catholic countries such as Italy or Spain differed both in its intent and in its sources of patronage from that of Protestant countries such as Holland or Britain, and it is partly because currents of classicism and naturalism coexisted with what is more narrowly defined as the High Baroque style.

The Baroque style in Italy and Spain had its origins in the last decades of the 16th century when the refined, courtly style of Mannerist painting had ceased to be an effective means of artistic expression. Indeed, Mannerism's inadequacy as a vehicle for religious art was being felt in artistic circles as early as the middle of that century. To counter the inroads made by the Reformation, the Roman Catholic Church after the Council of Trent (1545–63) adopted an overtly propagandistic stance in which the arts were intended to serve as a means of extending and stimulating the public's faith in the church and its doctrines. The church thus adopted a conscious artistic program, the products of which would make an overtly emotional and sensory appeal to the faithful. The Baroque style of painting that evolved from this program was paradoxically both sensuous and spiritual; while naturalistic treatment rendered the painted religious image more readily comprehensible to the average churchgoer, dramatic effects were used to stimulate piety and devotion. This appeal to the senses manifested itself in a style that above all emphasized movement and emotion. The stable, pyramidal compositions and clear, well-defined pictorial space characteristic of Renaissance paintings gave way in the Baroque to complex compositions surging along diagonal lines. The Baroque vision of the world is dynamic and dramatic; throngs of figures possessing a superabundant vitality energize the painted scene by means of their expressive gestures and movements. These figures are depicted with vividness and richness through the use of colours, dramatic effects of light and shade, and lavish use of highlights. The ceilings of Baroque churches thus dissolved in painted scenes that presented convincing views of the saints and angels to the observer and directed him through his senses to heavenly concerns.

EARLY AND HIGH BAROQUE IN ITALY

As early as the mid-16th century, a conscious reassessment of High Renaissance painting had begun to take place in Florence. This tendency gathered momentum in the last decades of the century. The Counter-Reformation reaffirmed the old medieval concept of art as the servant of the church, demanding simplicity, intelligibility, realism, and an emotional stimulus to piety. For the zealots of the Counter-Reformation, works of art had value only as propaganda material, the subject matter being all-important. In Rome there was consequentially a sharp decline in artistic quality. This late 16th-century style is best called Counter-Reformation Realist. Similar processes took place in Florence and Milan. In contrast, late 16th-century Venetian painting was as little influenced by the Counter-Reformation as it had been by Mannerism.

Michelangelo Merisi, better known by the name of his birthplace, Caravaggio, was active in Rome by about 1595. His earliest paintings are conspicuous for the almost enamel-like brilliance of the colours, the strong chiaroscuro called Tenebrism, and the extraordinary virtuosity with which all the details are rendered. But this harsh realism was replaced by a much more powerful mature style in his paintings for San Luigi dei Francesi, Rome, begun in 1597, and Santa Maria del Popolo, Rome, executed about 1601.

His selection of plebeian models for the most important characters in his religious pictures caused great controversy, but the utter sincerity of the figures and the intensity of dramatic feeling are characteristic of the Baroque. Although Caravaggio had no direct pupils, "Caravaggism" was the dominant new force in Rome during the first decade of the 17th century and subsequently had enormous influence outside Italy.

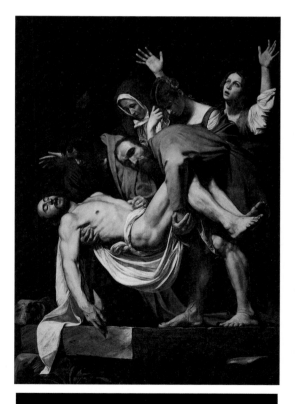

The Entombment of Christ, oil on canvas by Caravaggio, 1602–04; in the Vatican Museums, Vatican City

Parallel with Caravaggio's was the activity of Annibale Carracci in Rome. During Annibale's years in Bologna, he pioneered a synthesis of the traditionally opposed Renaissance concepts of *disegno* ("drawing") and *colore* ("colour"). In 1595 Carracci took to Rome his mature style, in which the plasticity of the central Italian tradition is wedded to the Venetian colour tradition. The decoration of the vault of the gallery in the Palazzo Farnese, Rome (1597–1604), marks not only the high point in Annibale's career but also the beginning of the long series of Baroque ceiling decorations. The third important painter active in Rome during the first decade of the 17th century was the Low Countries' painter Peter Paul Rubens, who became court painter to the duke of Mantua in 1600. The rich colours and strong dramatic chiaroscuro of his altarpieces for Santa Maria in Vallicella, Rome (1606–07), show his significant contribution to the evolution of Italian Baroque painting.

Just as the first decade tended to be dominated by the "Caravaggist" painters, the second decade in Rome was the heyday of the Bolognese classicist painters, who had been pupils of Annibale Carracci as well as his brother Agostino and his cousin Ludovico. The crucial developments that brought the High Baroque into being took place in the third decade.

The little church of Santa Bibiana in Rome harbours three of the key works that ushered in the High Baroque, all executed between 1624 and 1626: Gian Lorenzo Bernini's facade and the marble figure of Santa Bibiana herself, over the altar, and Pietro da Cortona's series of frescoes of Bibiana's life, painted on the side wall of the nave. The rich exuberance of the compositions is a prelude to the gigantic *Allegory of Divine Providence and Barberini Power*, which Pietro was to paint on the vault of the Great Hall of the Palazzo Barberini,

Allegory of Divine Providence and Barberini Power, fresco by Pietro da Cortona, 1633–39; in the Great Hall of the Palazzo Barberini, Rome

Rome (1633–39). Pietro continued with this style of monumental painting for the remainder of his career, and it became the model for the international grand decorative style.

Despite the continued triumph of High Baroque illusionism and theatricality in the hands of Bernini and Pietro from the 1630s, the forces of classicism gained the upper hand in the 1640s after the death of Pope Urban VIII.

For the remainder of the century the Baroque-versus-classicism controversy raged in the Academy in Rome. Andrea Sacchi and other classicists held that a scene must be depicted with a bare minimum of figures, each with its own clearly defined role, and compared the composition to that of a tragedy in literature. But Pietro and the Baroque camp held that the right parallel was the epic poem in which subsidiary episodes were added to give richness and variety to the whole, and hence the decorative richness and profusion of their great fresco cycles. A number of painters of importance did succeed in remaining more or less independent of the two main camps. Nonetheless, it was the Roman Baroque that dominated the first two-thirds of the 17th century in Italy.

The most conspicuous aspect of the last phase of the High Baroque in Italy is provided by the series of great fresco cycles, which were executed in Rome during the last decades of the 17th century. Pietro's decoration of Santa Maria in Vallicella (1647–55) is the link with the earlier phase of the Baroque, and his decoration of the gallery of the Palazzo Pamphili in Rome (1651–54) points the way to the later frescoes painted in other galleries and nave vaults throughout Italy. Concurrent with these fresco cycles, the Baroque-versus-classicism controversy took on a new lease on life, with Giovanni Battista Gaulli (Baciccio) heading the Baroque party in opposition to Sacchi's pupil Carlo Maratta. By the last decades of the century the Baroque was triumphant, and Maratta's Baroque classicism appears almost to be a compromise between Pietro and Sacchi.

The transition between the High Baroque and the Late Baroque was a continuous process and occurred at different dates with different artists. At Valmontone the sense of dynamic structure characteristic of the High Baroque frescoes of Pietro yields to a more decorative scheme in which the figures are scattered across the ceiling, giving the painting an overall unity without identifying any specific area as the focal point. The breakdown of any sense of direction in the composition is paralleled by a loosening in the design of individual figures; once again the unity is decorative rather than structural.

LATE BAROQUE AND ROCOCO

Symptomatic of the changing status of the papacy during the 17th century was the fact that the Thirty Years' War was ended by the Peace of Westphalia in 1648 without papal representation in the negotiations. Concurrently, the influence of Spain also declined. The commencement of the personal rule of Louis XIV in 1661 marked the beginning of a new era in French political power and artistic influence, and the French Academy in Rome (founded 1666) rapidly became a major factor in the evolution of Roman art. Late Baroque classicism, as represented in Rome by Maratta, was slowly transformed into a sweet and elegant 18th-century style by his pupil Benedetto Luti. Chiefly in Bologna and Venice, however, real attempts were made to break away from the confines of Late Baroque classicism.

Giuseppe Maria Crespi (called Lo Spagnolo, "The Spaniard") turned instead toward the early paintings of Guercino, an Italian painter whose frescoes had made a profound impact on 17th-century Baroque decoration. Crespi evolved a deeply sincere style, remarkable for its immediacy and sensibility. His work provided one of the bases for the brilliant flowering of Venetian painting in this period. While Giovanni Battista Piazzetta looked toward Crespi for the basis of his Tenebrist style, Sebastiano Ricci took his cue from Luca Giordano's frescoes. The brilliant lightness and vivacity of Ricci's frescoes in the Palazzo Marucelli-Fenzi, Florence, mark the beginning of a great tradition of Venetian decorative painting, a tradition that was to be carried all over Europe. The vast majority of the finest frescoes carried out by the Venetian 18th-century painters were executed outside the Veneto (the region of which Venice is the principal city), but the opposite is true of the flourishing Venetian school of landscape, *vedute* ("views"), and genre painters. Giovanni Antonio Canal, called Canaletto, developed these *vedute* into an industry almost entirely dependent upon foreign tourists. Francesco Guardi avoided the cool precision of Canaletto's *vedute* and instead evolved a much lighter and more lyrical Rococo style with a strong sense of the picturesque and, occasionally, the bizarre.

SPAIN AND PORTUGAL

Two fundamental and ostensibly opposed streams permeate Spanish painting and separate it from that of the rest of Europe— ecstatic mysticism and sober rationalism. These qualities are essentially Gothic in spirit, and the Iberian Peninsula is remarkable for the tenacity with which Gothic ideas were retained as well as for the relatively small influence of Renaissance humanist ideas. The early 17th-century still lifes of Sánchez Cotán, with their strong realism and harsh, mysterious lighting, illustrate these contrasts admirably, whereas Luis Tristán abandoned the Mannerist style for a much more careful realism.

One of the most important Spanish painters of the period was Diego Velázquez. From 1623 Velázquez's time was spent in the Spanish

Las Meninas, or *The Maids of Honor,* oil on canvas by Diego Velázquez, *c.* 1656; in the Prado Museum, Madrid. It includes a self-portrait of the artist at left, a reflection of King Philip IV and Queen Mariana in the mirror at the back of the artist's studio, and their daughter, the Infanta Margarita , and her *meninas,* or maids of honor, in the foreground.

court in Madrid. His early *bodegones* (scenes of daily life with strong elements of still life in the composition) were painted in Seville and belong to the Spanish realist tradition, but at court he saw the Titians collected by Philip II and also Rubens's paintings. After he visited Italy in 1629–31, there was greater freedom in the way he handled paint, more interest in colour, and increased depth to his analyses of character.

Other Spanish painters of the period generally followed the Spanish realist tradition. Many Spanish painters developed their own styles noted for gracefulness, and sentimentality. Particularly in Andalusia a liveliness of handling with accents of strong local colour replaced the sober realism popular in the first half of the century.

Portugal was ruled by Spain until 1640, when John IV was proclaimed king. But economic conditions hampered serious patronage of the arts until the reign of John V, when the most distinguished painter was Francisco Vieira de Matos. Unfortunately, the Lisbon earthquake of 1755 destroyed much of the best art collected in the Portuguese capital at that time.

LOW COUNTRIES

The year 1566 saw the Netherlands (then Spanish-held provinces) in open revolt against Philip II of Spain, and, inasmuch as this revolt had a Protestant as well as a nationalist aspect, a wave of iconoclasm swept across the area. By 1600 the area had become divided into the Spanish-dominated, Catholic, southern provinces—broadly modern Belgium—and the independent, predominantly Calvinist United Provinces of the north—broadly the modern Netherlands. In the southern provinces throughout the 16th to 18th centuries Brussels, headed by viceroys, remained the centre of court patronage, while Antwerp, with its great patrician families, was the commercial centre.

Painting in the southern provinces before 1610 was intensely conservative; the Mannerist conventions were never accepted as fully as in the north. Instead, Italianate ideas were joined with the late Gothic tradition.

In 1609 Peter Paul Rubens was appointed court painter with special permission to reside in Antwerp to help repair damage caused by the iconoclasm of 1566. The necessary ingredients were present for a brilliant flowering of the Baroque art that Rubens had evolved while in Italy, and his studio became an artistic centre not only for the Netherlands but for England, Spain, and central Europe as well. The monumentality of Rubens's forms, with their impulsive drawing, restless movement, and dramatic lighting, provided the touchstone for the High Baroque in the Catholic areas of northern Europe.

Anthony Van Dyck, a pupil and assistant of Rubens, was a much less forceful personality than his master. His paintings had a quieter, more introspective note than those of Rubens. Van Dyck was the most successful portrait painter of his time. Between 1625/26 and 1632 he was active, mainly as a portrait painter, in the entourage of Rubens, but the last years of his life (1632–41) were spent in England as court painter to Charles I. The elegant, relaxed, aristocratic portrait style he introduced was outstandingly successful.

One of the few painters of genius relatively independent of Rubens was Adriaen Brouwer, who painted in the tradition of Bruegel. Best known for his genre paintings, Brouwer also painted very expressive landscapes; his work is characterized by the sensitive use of a heavily loaded brush. In comparison, David Teniers the Younger was a minor master, and with him the influence of Dutch painting became increasingly strong. Still-life and animal painting reached new heights as a result of the influence of Rubens—a tradition that continued into the 18th century. Jan Davidsz de Heem was also active in Holland. He was a creator of the elaborate, fully developed Baroque still life. As such he had a host of followers and imitators.

Dutch painting of the 17th century shares roots with that of the Spanish Netherlands. Holland, however, was independent, rapidly prospering, and almost entirely Protestant. In the last decades of the 16th century the great port of Haarlem was the most active artistic centre, and the remarkable flowering of Mannerist painting there is without a parallel south of the border. Later Mannerism gave way to the much more straightforward realist style characteristic of the earliest phase of Dutch 17th-century painting. The influence of the figure paintings of Adam Elsheimer on this generation of artists was considerable. He had a particularly Italianate style, with sharply delineated forms painted in rich, deep colours and with a pronounced element of fantasy. Elsheimer's poetic little landscapes were also extremely important for the group of Dutch artists active in Rome about 1620. This group was headed by Cornelis van Poelenburgh and Bartolomeus Breenbergh, and back home it provided an additional source of Italian influence. The most striking influence of Italy was provided, however, by the Dutch followers of Caravaggio, who had seized eagerly upon the harsh dramatic lighting and coarse plebeian types they had seen in his paintings during their stays in Italy and brought the style to the north to form the so-called Utrecht school.

Rembrandt van Rijn evolved an increasingly Baroque style, with strong contrasts of light and shade derived from the "Caravaggists." After he moved to Amsterdam in 1631, these tendencies

UTRECHT SCHOOL

The Utrecht school was principally a group of three Dutch painters—Dirck van Baburen (*c.* 1590-1624), Gerrit van Honthorst (1590–1656), and Hendrik Terbrugghen (1588-1629)—who went to Rome and fell fully under the pervasive influence of Caravaggio's art before returning to Utrecht. Although none of them ever actually met Caravaggio (d. 1610), each had access to his paintings, knew his former patrons, and was influenced by the work of his follower Bartholomeo Manfredi (1580–1620/21), especially his half-length figural groups, which were boldly derived from Caravaggio and occasionally passed off as the deceased master's works.

Back in the Netherlands the "Caravaggisti" were eager to demonstrate what they had learned. Their subjects are frequently religious ones, but brothel scenes and pictures in sets, such as five works devoted to the senses, were popular with them also. The numerous candles, lanterns, and other sources of artificial light are characteristic and further underscore the indebtedness to Caravaggio.

developed to an opulent and highly Baroque climax in the late 1630s. Following the death of his first wife, Saskia, in 1642, difficult times and the changing tastes of art collectors culminated in his bankruptcy in 1656. In his later works the dramatic Baroque panache gives way to a deep introspection and sympathy for his subjects, and his series of about 60 self-portraits reveals this process in intimate detail. Parallel to his development as a painter is that of his style as an etcher; Rembrandt is considered by many to be the greatest etcher of all time. During the years of his financial success, Rembrandt had the largest and most successful painting and printmaking studio in Holland.

The increasing use at this time of portable easel paintings as domestic ornaments is related to the extraordinary range of subjects in which Dutch painters specialized. Nevertheless, certain basic changes in style and taste occurred during the course of the 17th century, and, although many painters long persisted in outdated styles, the same fundamental changes can be traced in the various specialties. The earliest phase of simple realism held sway until the early 1620s; in the work of several artists were to be found the characteristic bright local colours, lack of spatial unity, sudden transition between different planes, and tendency toward high viewpoints. This gave way to a much more limited palette in the early 1620s when, by reducing the strength and range of the colours, an atmospheric unity was obtained. In landscapes and marine paintings the horizon tended to drop, and a continuous and coherent recession into depth was attained. The same change is seen in still lifes, where the colours became almost monochrome. Atmospheric unity having been mastered, the change to the heroic classical phase of the middle of the 17th century was gradual, but there was a tendency toward ever-increasingly dramatic Baroque contrasts. The monumentality of these scenes is paralleled by a rich splendour in still lifes. In some artists, the majesty of Jacob van Ruisdael's landscapes gives way to a much lighter, more picturesque style.

With the French invasion of 1672 and the subsequent Dutch economic collapse, the demand for paintings dropped heavily, and in the last decades of the 17th century many Dutch painters either stopped painting or left the country to work in England or Germany.

FRANCE

French-speaking painters continued the Mannerist conventions even later than did those at Haarlem, and at Nancy, a group of artists around Jacques Bellange and Jacques

Callot was responsible for the last great flowering of the Mannerist style in Europe. By comparison, painting in Paris during the first decades of the 17th century was relatively insignificant. The return of Simon Vouet to Paris, however, marked the arrival of the Baroque in France. The earliest paintings from his stay in Rome are strikingly vigorous essays in the "Caravaggesque" style, but by 1620 he was painting in an eclectic, classicizing style based on the early Baroque painters active there. This style he brought back to France, enjoying until his death an immense success in Paris as a decorator and painter of large-scale altarpieces.

The influence of the highly Baroque paintings depicting the life of Marie de Médicis that Rubens had executed for the Luxembourg Palace in Paris was small. But Philippe de Campaigne evolved a grave and sober Baroque style that had its roots in the paintings of Rubens and Van Dyck rather than in Italy. Clear lighting and cool colours with an austere naturalism provided an alternative to the intellectual and archaeological classicism of other French artists. Indeed many French painters of the period look to Dutch painting— and especially the Utrecht School—for their inspiration.

In the reorganization of the Academy of Painting and Sculpture in 1648, Charles Le Brun was appointed director and given the position of virtual dictator of the arts in France. An imaginative painter and designer, Le Brun was also a brilliant organizer, and the creation of the Louis XIV style, as exemplified by the Palace of Versailles, was above all due to him. The particular Baroque style that emerged was based on the Roman High Baroque but was purged of all theatricality and illusionism and modified to conform to the classical canons of French taste. During the last decades of the century, the full Baroque style took on a new vigour. Decorative paintings of the period clearly reveal the influence of Rubens. The formal portraits by Hyacinthe Rigaud and Nicolas de Largillière are firmly Baroque. Their strong *contrapposto*, rich settings, and floating masses of drapery reflect the pomp and swagger of this era—which, significantly, came to be known as the Grande Époque.

The great formal portraits of Rigaud and Largillière are entirely Baroque in their approach, but in the late informal portraits of these masters a new atmosphere called Rococo prevails. The turn of the century marks the victory of Rubens's influence over severe classicism. The evolution of the Rococo style of decoration has been traced from its emergence at the beginning of the 18th century, and it must be emphasized that the Rococo is fundamentally a decorative style. It made relatively little impact on religious painting in France. It took the genius of

Antoine Watteau to put together all the ideas current in Paris and to create the new style of painting. Watteau's painting demonstrated a delicate sketchlike technique and included elegant figures of the artist's wistful fantasies, called *fêtes galantes*. Paintings that displayed eroticism and an amorous dalliance formed an intimate part of the decoration of Rococo interiors. More than any earlier secular paintings they were intended as a kind of two-dimensional furniture.

The furniture role also applies to the paintings of dead game and live dogs by François Desportes and Jean-Baptiste Oudry. But in the still lifes and tranquil scenes of domestic life painted by Jean-Baptiste-Siméon Chardin there is a sobriety of colour and composition, an often relatively homely subject matter, and a concern to order the mind rather than dazzle the eye. Some of Chardin's subjects—the labours of the servant

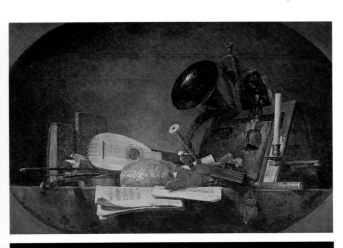

The Attributes of Music, oil on canvas by Jean-Baptiste-Siméon Chardin, 1765; in the Louvre, Paris

class, the care of children—were shared by Jean-Baptiste Greuze, who was, however, more interested in narrative and sentiment. Unlike Dutch painters of lower-class life, Greuze endowed his peasants with the sensibility of their social superiors.

Despite his great success, Greuze was judged to have failed in his attempt at painting heroic narrative from ancient history. But then it is true that the "higher" class of painting was generally less successfully practiced in France than were the "lower" genres in the 18th century.

The middle decades of the 18th century saw more accomplished portrait painters flourishing in France than perhaps ever before in any country. Yet the portraiture of these decades is associated with the informal, the convivial, and the intimate. The heroic was seldom attempted and never achieved.

BRITAIN

During the 17th century English painting had been dominated by a series of foreign-born practitioners, mostly portraitists (such as Rubens and Van Dyck). Sir Peter Lely and Sir Godfrey Kneller continued this trend after the Restoration. The vast majority of the painting executed by native artists remained thoroughly provincial. Lely began his activity in England during the Civil War, probably in

1641, but his portraits of the members of the court of Charles II set the pattern for English portraiture of the second half of the 17th century. British patrons in the 18th century sometimes collected paintings on religious or mythical themes by foreign artists, but at home they rarely commissioned anything other than portraits, landscapes, and marine paintings, although there was in the early 18th century a vogue for grand allegorical decorations in aristocratic houses. The Protestant church, however, did little to encourage painting. In fact, the preponderance of portraits is the most distinctive characteristic of old British collections.

The Glorious Revolution of 1688 was followed by a brief flowering of decorative painting under Sir James Thornhill, which was the closest that Britain ever approached to the developed Baroque style of the Continent. This process was in part due to the influx, following the end of the War of the Spanish Succession, of Italian and French painters. The German-born Kneller succeeded Lely as court portrait painter, but, although his portraits often have a certain liveliness, his rather heavy use of studio assistants resulted in a tendency to monotony.

Thornhill's son-in-law William Hogarth was heavily influenced by the continental Rococo style. Early in his career he succeeded in breaking away from the straitjacket of portraiture, and his moralizing paintings are superb evocations of life in the England of George I and George II. His rich, creamy paint handling and brilliant characterization of textures have a freshness and vitality unequaled in the work of any of his contemporaries. He invented a new form of secular narrative painting that imparts a moral. These paintings were often tragicomedies, although dependent upon no texts, and Hogarth's series of such works were always intended to be engraved for a large public as well as seen in a private picture gallery.

Despite Hogarth's considerable knowledge of and borrowings from continental old masters, he remained in the last analysis English through and through. This, however, was not the case with all the next generation of painters. The Scottish-born Allan Ramsay studied in Rome and Naples in 1736–38 before settling in London in 1739. In the 1740s Ramsay held undisputed sway as the most successful portrait painter in London, and to him must be given the credit for the initial marriage of the Italian "grand style" to English portraiture. English artist Sir Joshua Reynolds, who had spent two years in Italy, possessed great ambitions and a more profound acquaintance with the old masters than any of his contemporaries. His colouring and handling can be compared with Rembrandt, Rubens, and Veronese, and his poses are indebted to the sculpture of antiquity and to

Michelangelo. The *Discourses* that he delivered to the Royal Academy (founded in 1768 with Reynolds as its first president) are the most impressive statement in English of the central ideas of European art theory since the time of Alberti's *De pictura* treatise.

The third major British painter of the period to study in Italy was a Welshman, Richard Wilson, who worked there from 1750 to about 1757 before settling in London. The clear golden lighting of his Italian landscapes carries the conviction of an artist saturated with the Mediterranean tradition. A cooler clarity and classical simplicity pervade his northern landscapes; and, despite the uneven quality of his work, Wilson was the first British painter to lift the pure landscape above mere decorative painting and topography.

Thomas Gainsborough was in every way the antithesis to Reynolds. Trained entirely in England, he had no wish to visit Italy. Instead of the "grand style," his tastes in portraiture lay in the delicate flickering brushwork and evanescent qualities of the Rococo. He preferred landscape painting to portraiture, and the strong Dutch influence in his earliest works later gave way to spontaneous landscapes composed from models.

Throughout the 18th century, portraiture remained the most important genre of British painting, despite the efforts of Reynolds and Gainsborough. Even the taste for large-scale scenes illustrating Shakespeare and other themes never spread far beyond a few patrons.

THE BAROQUE IN THE NEW WORLD

Painting in the Dutch and English colonies of North America reflected generally the portrait styles of the mother countries, though with a note of provinciality. In the late 17th and early 18th centuries the Dutch colony of New Amsterdam (New York) had painters whose names today are forgotten. Their work lives on, however, and is signified by names such as the Master of the De Peyster Boy.

Baroque painting in Central and South America is basically an extension of that of Spain and Portugal, and even the best rarely rises to the general standard of the European schools. Important paintings and sculptures tended to be imported from Europe, and the Spanish painter Francisco de Zurbarán was particularly active in producing works for export, while local productions were more or less heavily influenced by the Indian traditions.

During the second half of the 18th century the evolution of British oil painting was to a great extent paralleled by an extraordinary flowering in watercolours.

CENTRAL EUROPE

In central Europe the Mannerist tradition remained dominant until the Thirty Years' War, particularly in Bohemia and Bavaria, where Italian influence was perhaps strongest.

The Rubensian Baroque became dominant after mid-century, and here the lead was taken by Silesia and Bohemia. The vast majority of the best central European Baroque painting outside portraiture is monumental in scale, and the concept of the *Gesamtkunstwerk* ("total work of art")—where painting, sculpture, and architecture are combined together into a single, unified, and harmonious ensemble—is of overwhelming importance.

Painting in Austria flourished, and Franz Anton Maulbertsch is arguably the greatest painter of the 18th century in central Europe. The vast majority of his brilliant fresco cycles are located in relatively inaccessible areas of Bohemia, Moravia, and northern Hungary. But the mystical intensity of his religious scenes and the joyous abandon of his secular subjects form a triumphant closing chapter to 18th-century central European painting. The Neoclassicism that descended in the last decades of the 18th century had an impact on all Austrian painters. However, Austrian monumental painting remained fully Baroque in the hands of certain artists, and it was not until the latter part of the century that the Rococo made its impact.

During the first four decades of the 18th century, Bohemian Baroque painting developed almost independently of Vienna, where the Habsburg rulers of Bohemia had their capital. The impetuous work of Jan Petr Brandl and the powerful realism of the portraitist Jan Kupecký, who worked in Rome, Venice, Vienna, and Nürnberg, always remained Bohemian in spirit. The influence of Bohemian Baroque painting is frequently underestimated. Apart from Vienna and the surrounding area, it was dominant in Silesia and strong later in the century in Franconia.

The centre of south German painting shifted by the late 1730s from Munich to Augsburg. The second half of the 18th century witnessed a shift from the Rococo to Neoclassicism.

CHAPTER SIX

THE NEOCLASSICAL AND ROMANTIC PERIODS

The 18th-century arts movement known as Neoclassicism represents both a reaction against the last phase of the Baroque and, perhaps more importantly, a reflection of the burgeoning scientific interest in classical antiquity. Neoclassicism sought to revive those characteristics normally associated with the aesthetics of antiquity that invoke harmony, clarity, universality, and idealism. Through much of its later development, Neoclassicism coexisted with Romanticism. Romanticism rejected the precepts of order, calm, harmony, balance, idealization, and rationality, all of which typified classicism in general and Neoclassicism in particular. The aesthetics of Romanticism focus instead on visually expressing and igniting individual emotion.

NEOCLASSICISM

Neoclassicism was a widespread and influential movement in visual arts that began in the 1760s and reached its height in the 1780s and '90s. It lasted until the 1840s and '50s. In painting it generally took the form of an emphasis on austere linear design in the depiction of classical themes and subject matter, using archaeologically correct settings and costumes.

Neoclassicism arose partly as a reaction against the sensuous and frivolously decorative Rococo style. But an even more profound stimulus was the new and more scientific interest in classical antiquity that arose in the 18th century. Neoclassicism was given great impetus by new archaeological discoveries, particularly the exploration and excavation of the buried Roman cities of Herculaneum and Pompeii (which began in 1738 and 1748, respectively). And from the second decade of the 18th century on, a number of influential publications provided engraved views of Roman monuments and other antiquities, further quickening interest in the classical past. The new understanding distilled from these discoveries and publications in turn enabled

European scholars for the first time to discern separate and distinct chronological periods in Greco-Roman art. The German scholar Johann Joachim Winckelmann's writings and sophisticated theorizing were especially

JOHANN WINCKELMANN

Johann Winckelmann (b. Dec. 9, 1717, Stendal, Prussia–d. June 8, 1768, Trieste) was a German archaeologist and art historian whose writings directed popular taste toward classical art, particularly that of ancient Greece, and influenced not only Western painting and sculpture but also literature and even philosophy.

Winckelmann's *History of the Art of Antiquity* (1764) was probably the first work to define the development of ancient art in its own environment, as it proceeded from birth through maturity to decline. The book also inaugurated the division of ancient art into periods. Winckelmann's fame, however, rests on his meticulous descriptions of specific works of art.

The genius and writings of Winckelmann, more than of any other single critic, reawakened the popular taste for classical art and were instrumental in generating the Neoclassical movement in the arts.

influential in this regard. Winckelmann saw in Greek sculpture "a noble simplicity and quiet grandeur" and called for artists to imitate Greek art. He claimed that in doing so such artists would obtain idealized depictions of natural forms that had been stripped of all transitory and individualistic aspects, and their images would thus attain a universal and archetypal significance.

Neoclassicism as manifested in painting was initially not stylistically distinct from the French Rococo and other styles that had preceded it. This was partly because, whereas it was possible for architecture and sculpture to be modeled on prototypes in these media that had actually survived from classical antiquity, those few classical paintings that had survived were minor or merely ornamental works—until, that is, the discoveries made at Herculaneum and Pompeii. The earliest Neoclassical painters were Joseph-Marie Vien, Anton Raphael Mengs, Pompeo Batoni, Angelica Kauffmann, and Gavin Hamilton; these artists were active during the 1750s, '60s, and '70s. Though they may have used poses and figural arrangements from ancient sculptures and vase paintings, the earliest Neoclassical painters were strongly influenced by preceding stylistic trends.

A more rigorously Neoclassical painting style arose in France in the 1780s under the leadership of Jacques-Louis David. He and his contemporary Jean-François-Pierre Peyron were interested in narrative painting rather than the ideal grace that fascinated Mengs. Just before and during the French Revolution, these and other painters adopted stirring moral subject matter from Roman history and celebrated the values of simplicity, austerity, heroism, and stoic virtue that were traditionally associated with the Roman Republic, thus drawing parallels between that time and the contemporary struggle for liberty in France. David's history paintings of the *Oath of the Horatii* (1784) and *Lictors Bringing to Brutus the Bodies of His Sons* (1789) display a gravity and decorum deriving from classical tragedy, a certain rhetorical quality of gesture, and patterns of drapery influenced by ancient sculpture. In David's works can be seen a dramatic confrontations of figures and more monumental settings, and the diagonal compositional movements, large groupings of figures, and turbulent draperies of the Baroque have been almost entirely repudiated. This style

was ruthlessly austere and uncompromising, and it is not surprising that it came to be associated with the French Revolution (in which David actively participated).

Lictors Bringing to Brutus the Bodies of His Sons, oil on canvas by Jacques-Louis David, 1789; in the Louvre, Paris

Neoclassicism as generally manifested in European painting by the 1790s emphasized the qualities of outline and linear design over those of colour, atmosphere, and effects of light. Widely disseminated engravings of classical sculptures and Greek vase paintings helped determine this bias. Neoclassical painters attached great importance to depicting the costumes, settings, and details of their classical subject matter with as much historical accuracy as possible.

Classical history and mythology provided a large part of the subject matter of Neoclassical works. The poetry of Homer, Virgil, and Ovid, the plays of Aeschylus, Sophocles, and Euripides, and history recorded by Pliny, Plutarch, Tacitus, and Livy provided the bulk of classical sources, but the most important single source was Homer. To this general literary emphasis was added a growing interest in medieval sources as well as incidents from medieval history, the works of Dante, and an admiration for medieval art itself. Indeed, the Neoclassicists differed strikingly from their academic predecessors in their admiration of Gothic art in general, and they contributed notably to the positive reevaluation of such art.

Finally, it should be noted that Neoclassicism coexisted throughout much of its later development with the seemingly obverse and opposite tendency of Romanticism. But far from being distinct and separate, these two styles intermingled with each other in complex ways; many ostensibly Neoclassical paintings show Romantic tendencies, and vice versa.

ROMANTICISM

"Romanticism" is a term loosely used to designate numerous and diverse changes in the arts during a period lasting roughly from 1760 until 1870. These changes were in reaction against Neoclassicism (although not necessarily the classicism of Greece and Rome) or against the Enlightenment and 18th-century materialism. In the sense of a personal temperament, Romanticism had always existed, but in the sense of an aesthetic period it signified works of art whose prime impulse and effect derived from individual rather than collective reactions. Romanticism can generally be said to have emphasized the personal, the subjective, the irrational, the imaginative, the spontaneous, the emotional, and even the visionary and transcendental in works of art. The Romantic movement first developed in northern Europe with a rejection of technical standards based on the classical ideal that perfection should be attained in art.

It was writers and poets who gave initial expression to Romantic ideas; painters, while subject to similar feelings, acquired fundamental inspiration from the literature of the period. There was an increasing awareness generally of the way the various arts interacted. The Frenchman Eugène Delacroix and the German Philipp Otto Runge explored the implications of musical analogies for painting, and everywhere writers, artists, and composers could be found in close association.

Romantic critics agreed that experience of profound inner emotion was the mainspring of creation and appreciation of art. Received ideas, and especially aesthetic values sanctioned by the authority of official institutions, were distrusted, and the individual was pitted against society. The artist asserted the right to evolve his own criteria of beauty and in so doing encouraged a new concept of artistic genius. The genius celebrated by the Romantics was one who refused to conform, who remained defiantly independent of society, and whose chief virtues were novelty and sincerity. This sometimes led to bizarre and extravagant projects in which the intention to shock, excite, and involve struck a melodramatic, almost hysterical note that failed to convince by its very lack of restraint.

As in the literature of the period, tragic themes predominated in Romantic painting, and interest turned sharply from classical history and mythology to medieval subjects, although an interest in the primitive was sometimes common to both. The fascination with the Middle Ages combined with strong nationalist tendencies, disposing artists to a concern with the history and folklore of their own countries. At the same time they often sought themes or styles that were distant in place as well as time. Accounts of foreign travel and literary works greatly influenced painters. Study of medieval culture imbued some painters with a Christian ideal of simplicity and moral integrity.

A salient feature of Romantic sensibility was awareness of the beauties of the natural world. Artists identified their personal feelings with nature's changing aspects. An almost reverential affection, animated by the belief that the divine mind was immanent in nature, engendered at times a Christian or theistic naturalism. The artist was seen as the interpreter of hidden mysteries, to which end imaginative insight must combine with absolute fidelity and sincerity. In Britain and Germany especially, the moral implications inherent in the appreciation of natural or artistic beauty tended to outweigh aesthetic considerations. Interest in transitory phenomena led painters to devote themselves to an accurate study of light and atmosphere and their effects on the landscape. Concern to preserve the spontaneity of the immediate impression brought about a revolution in painterly technique, with the rapid notation of the sketch carried into the final conception. Whether emphasizing expressive or purely visual considerations, the landscape paintings of the period display dazzling colour.

Curiosity about the external world and a spirit of what might be called scientific inquiry led many painters to explore the minutiae of nature. Technological advance also excited artistic interest, though painting was affected less than architecture and the decorative arts; and the humanitarian sympathy and generosity so vital to the Romantic spirit gradually effected a reconciliation between art and life. The political and social upheavals of the 19th century involved many painters in revolutionary movements and stimulated a solicitude toward the helpless and downtrodden that found most passionate and powerful expression in the works executed during and immediately after the Revolutions of 1848.

GERMANY

In Germany also there was a reaction against classicism and the academies, and, as elsewhere, it involved all aspects of the arts. Again, as elsewhere, theory preceded practice: *Herzensergiessungen eines kunstliebenden Klosterbruders* (`Effusions of an Art-Loving Monk"), by Wilhelm Heinrich Wackenroder, had an immediate and widespread influence upon its publication in 1797. Wackenroder advocated a Christian art closely related to the art of the early German masters and provided the artist with a new role as interpreter of divine inspiration through his own feelings.

The painter Philipp Otto Runge had been reared on 17th-century German mysticism, and he proved susceptible to the ideas of writers such as Wackenroder. In Dresden he formed a close association with the leading German landscape painter Caspar David Friedrich. Like Friedrich he was fascinated by the potential symbolic and allegorical power of landscape, which he used as a vehicle for religious expression. His vision of nature was pantheistic, and in his portraits his aim was to capture the soul of the individual as part of the universal soul of nature. His interest in the German past, including folklore and fairy tales, was reflected in a bizarre fairylike quality in much of his work.

Whereas Runge, Friedrich, and their followers interpreted Wackenroder in a highly personal way, others were inspired to communal activity. A number of young painters in Vienna founded in 1809 a group they called the Guild of St. Luke. The founding members were Johann Friedrich Overbeck (their leader), Franz Pforr,

THE NAZARENES

The Nazarenes were members of the Guild of Saint Luke (German *Nazarener*, or *Lukasbund*), an association formed by a number of young German painters in 1809 to return to the medieval spirit in art. Reacting particularly against 18th-century Neoclassicism, the brotherhood was the first effective antiacademic movement in European painting. The Nazarenes believed that all art should serve a moral or religious purpose; they admired painters of the late Middle Ages and early Renaissance and rejected most subsequent painting (promulgated by the European academies), believing that it abandoned religious ideals in favour of artistic virtuosity. They also thought that the mechanical routine of the academy system could be avoided by a return to the more intimate teaching situation of the medieval workshop. For this reason, they worked and lived together in a semimonastic existence.

The art of the Nazarenes, consisting largely of religious subjects executed in a conventional naturalistic style, was, for the most part, unimpressive, characterized by overcrowded compositions, overattention to detail, and lack of colouristic vitality. Nevertheless, their aim of honest expression of deeply felt ideals had an important influence on subsequent movements, particularly the English Pre-Raphaelites.

Joseph Wintergerst, Joseph Sutter, and Georg Ludwig Vogel. In 1810 they moved to Rome, and the group expanded. Their semimonastic existence occasioned the nickname Nazarenes.

BRITAIN

In the late 1760s and '70s a number of British artists at home and in Rome, including James Barry, Henry Fuseli, John Hamilton Mortimer, and John Flaxman, began to paint subjects that were at odds with the strict decorum and classical historical and mythological subject matter of conventional figurative art. These artists favoured themes that were bizarre, pathetic, or extravagantly heroic, and they defined their images with tensely linear drawing and bold contrasts of light and shade.

William Blake, the other principal early Romantic painter in England, evolved his own powerful and unique visionary

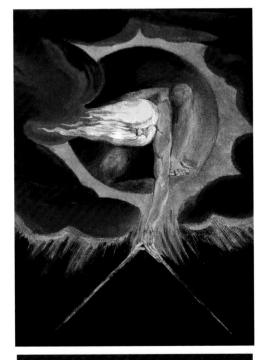

The Ancient of Days, watercolour and relief etching by William Blake, *c.* 1794; this copy is in the Glasgow University Library, Glasgow

images. Blake rejected oils in favour of tempera and watercolour, and depicted, as in *Pity* (1795), a shadowless world of soaring, supernatural beings. His passionate rejection of rationalism and materialism stemmed from a conviction that "poetic genius" could alone perceive the infinite, so essential to the artist since "painting, as well as poetry and music, exists and exults in immortal thoughts."

Empiricism and acceptance of the irrational, however, were not mutually exclusive, and each profoundly affected attitudes toward nature. Susceptible to the ideas of Blake and other radical theorists and animated by a growing spirit of inquiry into natural phenomena, painters slowly abandoned the picturesque desire to compose and became willing to be moved, awestruck, and terrified by nature unadorned. Early artists of the sublime worked largely in watercolours and solved the problem of scale by abstraction—use of broad areas of colour to suggest the vast scope of natural forces.

By the early 19th century, the great genre of English Romantic landscape painting emerged in the works of J.M.W. Turner and John Constable. These artists emphasized transient and dramatic effects of light, atmosphere, and colour to portray a dynamic natural world capable of evoking awe and grandeur. Both men believed that personal feeling was the mainspring of artistic activity and felt an almost mystical sympathy for the natural world. They made atmosphere almost palpable and painted everything from clouds to lichens with astonishing technical diversity.

The Pre-Raphaelite Brotherhood— formed by Dante Gabriel Rossetti, William Holman Hunt, and John Everett Millais in 1848—echoed that of the German Nazarenes (a group of religiously minded painters who sought to revive medieval workshop practices) and reiterated many earlier Romantic ideals. Literary inspiration and a passion for the Middle Ages were tempered for the Pre-Raphaelites by a moral outlook that recoiled from sophistication and virtuosity and demanded rigorous studies from natural life. These painters handled literary, historical, biblical, and contemporary themes with the same sincerity and fidelity that yielded the sparkling precision of Pre-Raphaelite landscape. Their earnest pursuit of truth entailed a denial of many orthodox artistic pleasures. Together with Ford Madox Brown, the Pre-Raphaelites sustained the devotion to colour and light in painting that underlies the finest endeavours of English Romanticism.

FRANCE

The French Revolution greatly stimulated interest in the depiction of contemporary events. Encouraged by David's example, painters in France sought to represent authentically the crucial moments of their own time. Napoleon I enthusiastically endorsed this awareness of modern heroism and demanded pictorial celebration of the glorious achievements of the empire. After the fall of Napoleon, however, few were disposed to depict contemporary subjects.

The chief early Romantic painters in France were Baron Antoine Gros, who painted dramatic tableaus of contemporary incidents of the Napoleonic Wars, and Théodore Géricault, whose depictions of individual heroism and suffering in *The Raft of the Medusa* (1819) and in his portraits of the insane truly inaugurated the movement around 1820.

The French Romantic painter often considered the greatest was Eugène Delacroix. The paintings of Delacroix frequently disrupted the salons of the 1820s and '30s with their tumultuous colour and emotive energy. His fertile imagination, embracing a novel range of literary and historical themes and fastening with a characteristic sense of the sadness of life on moments of death, defeat, and suffering, together with his prodigious technical resources exemplify Romanticism in its most obvious aspects. His vigorous handling of paint and expert use of colour values for both description and expression were important for the later development of French painting. *The Massacre at Chios* (1824) transposes

Liberty Leading the People, oil on canvas by Eugène Delacroix, 1830; in the Louvre, Paris

contemporary events into a realm of tragic fiction soon established unrestrainedly with such melodramatic works as *The Death of Sardanapalus* (1827), a riot of brilliant colour and ebullient forms.

Delacroix's Moroccan paintings released a flood of North African subjects, but Delacroix was not the first to handle Oriental subjects. Jean-Auguste-Dominique Ingres had already done so with a reticence that belies the sensuous delight in such works as *Valpinçon Bather* (1808) and *La Grande Odalisque* (1814). Early in his career Ingres made notable contributions to the historical genre with episodes from medieval French history painted in a style of linear purity that parallels the methods of Flaxman and Blake in Britain and the Nazarenes in Germany. Under the spell of Raphael he returned to the academic fold, but his portraits always retained that trenchant simplicity and lucid insight that make him such a memorable exponent of lyric realism.

The career of Ingres and in a converse sense that of Paul Delaroche well illustrate the imprudence of too readily distinguishing between academic and Romantic artists. Delaroche, perhaps the most popular representative of the Romantic school, specialized in highly charged narratives with royal and child characters, of which *The Children of Edward* (*c.* 1830) is a typical example, being executed with a flatness that lacks either linear or colouristic inspiration. In comparison, the work of Théodore Chassériau is animated by powerful emotional overtones reminiscent of Delacroix. *The Cossack Girl Finding the Body of Mazeppa* (1851) shows a similarly expressive use of paint, together with poignant imagery, both characteristic of his regrettably slender oeuvre. At the end of the century, Gustave Moreau and Odilon Redon transformed these features, along with others in Louis Boulanger's work, into whimsical, haunting fantasies that delighted the Symbolist poets.

In the 1830s and '40s it was Honoré Daumier, more than any other artist, who portrayed relatively lowly members of society, expressing in numerous drawings and paintings their patient resignation. In contrast, his truly excoriating depiction of the weaknesses and vices of the privileged classes, particularly officialdom, often displeased authority, which had long identified Romanticism with liberalism—and with good reason. A strain of poetic realism in the 1840s, essentially Romantic in approach, gathered sudden momentum with the Revolution and short-lived republic of 1848. Jean-François Millet and Gustave Courbet depicted peasant life, investing it with a certain timeless quality.

A new approach to the familiar and unsophisticated occurs in the landscape painting of the 1830s and '40s. French Romanticism gave rise to the Barbizon school, a group of naturalist painters who were particularly active in the forest of Fontainebleau. In this period the charm of the spontaneous sketch as opposed to the finished study was recognized: painters readily set up their easels in the open air and scrutinized the scene before them. A direct approach to nature and an interest in transitory moments, especially the changing effects of light, were features common to Romantic landscape painters throughout Europe and the United States. The changed attitude to landscape is aptly expressed in the work of Théodore Rousseau. Rousseau attempted to render nature as he found it, though his melancholic temperament is inevitably reflected in the desolate panoramas and gloomy sunsets in which he expressed an almost pantheistic feeling for the natural world. At the same time, his close attention to detail and painstaking accuracy in the delineation of plants and grasses betray the scientific concern shared by many Romantic artists.

While they laid the foundation for the painterly revolution of the Impressionists, the Barbizon painters always retained the generous appreciation of natural beauty and emotional involvement with their subject that everywhere distinguish the Romantic temperament.

UNITED STATES

American Romantic painters were largely influenced by trends in late 18th-century Europe, especially Britain, but the absence of an indigenous artistic tradition permitted a much more intuitive development. At the same time, their work, like that of the early French Romantics, is closely associated with the new spirit fostered by a national revolution. The American Revolution, by reinforcing the democratic ideal, inspired a unique brand of Romantic realism that was a strong force in American painting from the late 18th century onward and that anticipated the emergence in Europe by a whole generation. John Trumbull undertook a series of 12 scenes from the American Revolution, in which careful studies of the principal participants were incorporated into colourful, baroque compositions. In 1784 one of the most candid portraitists of the period, Charles Willson Peale, completed a similarly ambitious project in his paintings of the leading figures of the Revolution. At the beginning of the Romantic period, artists were still influenced by British painting, but this influence grew less and less perceptible as the 19th century progressed.

The career of the landscape painter Washington Allston reflects the development of American painting in his lifetime. Absorbed by German and English Romantic poetry, he began on a note of high drama, moving in cosmopolitan artistic circles in Rome and producing a number of early landscapes. At this point, what was obviously an impetuous and brooding strain in Allston's temperament found expression by depicting nature in the darker, more destructive moods dear to Turner. *The Deluge* (1804) is a typical macabre invention, with bodies in a raging tempest swept ashore to where wolves and serpents lurk. On his return to the United States, however, his work assumed a quieter, more pensive aspect.

THE HUDSON RIVER SCHOOL

The Hudson River school was a large group of American landscape painters of several generations who worked between about 1825 and 1870. The name, applied retrospectively, refers to a similarity of intent rather than to a geographic location, though many of the older members of the group drew inspiration from the picturesque Catskill region north of New York City, through which the Hudson River flows. An outgrowth of the Romantic movement, the Hudson River school was the first native school of painting in the United States; it was strongly nationalistic both in its proud celebration of the natural beauty of the American landscape and in the desire of its artists to become independent of European schools of painting.

The early leaders of the Hudson River school were Thomas Doughty, Asher Durand, and Thomas Cole, all of whom worked in the open and painted reverential, carefully observed pictures of untouched wilderness in the Hudson River valley and nearby locations in New England. Although these painters and most of the others who followed their example studied in Europe at some point, all had first achieved a measure of success at home and had established the common theme of the remoteness and splendour of the American interior. Doughty concentrated on serene, lyrical, contemplative scenes of the valley itself. Durand, also lyrical, was more intimate and particularly made use of delicate lighting in woodland scenes. Cole, the most romantic of the early group, favoured the stormy and monumental aspects of nature. Other painters who concentrated on depicting the landscape of the northeastern United States were Alvan Fisher, Henry Inman, and Samuel F.B. Morse and, later, John Kensett, John Casilear, Worthington Whittredge, and Jasper F. Cropsey.

For some painters whose theme was untouched landscape, the Northeast was less alluring than the more primitive and dramatic landscapes of the West. John Banvard and Henry Lewis painted huge panoramas of empty stretches of the Mississippi River. Among the first artists to explore the far West were the enormously successful Thomas Moran and Albert Bierstadt, who painted grandiose scenes of the Rocky Mountains, the Grand Canyon, and Yosemite Valley. The Hudson River school remained the dominant school of American landscape painting throughout most of the 19th century.

An uncomplicated love for their own natural scenery emerges in the work of a succession of landscape painters who frequently strike a contemplative, lyrical note. Thomas Cole reverently recorded scenes in the valley of the Hudson River that echo the loneliness and mystery of the North American forests. Simplicity and reticence distinguish the landscapes of Thomas Doughty, who

Fur Traders Descending the Missouri, oil on canvas by George Caleb Bingham, 1845; in the Metropolitan Museum of Art, New York

also concentrated on painting the Hudson River valley as he knew and loved it. The details of country life are portrayed with affection by William Sidney Mount, who in *Eel Spearing at Setauket* (1845) transcends the merely anecdotal. George Caleb Bingham approached the life of the frontier without the passionate concern that motivated many contemporary French artists. Solemn and severe in style and glowing with colour, his *Fur Traders Descending the Missouri* (1845) captures the silence and solitary grandeur of frontier life. The wildness of the frontier caught the imagination of many 19th-century artists, who discovered a picturesque drama and excitement in Indian life. The Romantic period witnessed the emergence of a truly national school of painting in the United States, where events and scenery provided a constant source of stimulation for artists content to distill their own poetry from the world around them.

RUSSIA

Napoleon's invasion of Russia (1812) had far-reaching consequences. It marked the revival of national consciousness and the beginning of a widespread cult of Russian separateness from Europe, thus precipitating the long controversy between "Westerners" and "Slavophiles" that ran through so much of Russian 19th-century literature and thought. At the same time, Russia shared in the Romanticism—cultivated by France and Germany—that gripped Europe during the era of the Napoleonic Wars. The most notable contribution to the Romantic spirit was made by Karl Pavlovich Bryullov, with his monumental painting *The Last Days of Pompeii* (1830–33). A completely different trend appears in the work of Aleksandr Ivanov, the first Russian painter to express religious emotions in a western European manner. Other outstanding artists of that period were Aleksey Venetsianov and Pavel Fedotov, the forerunners of Realist painting in Russia.

The second half of the 19th century saw the maturing of Realism in Russia. A sympathetic attitude toward the hard life of the people is reflected in the works of most of the painters and sculptors of that time. The new trend in art had as its basis the populist revolutionary ferment prevalent toward the end of the 1850s and the beginning of the 1860s, much of it inspired by the writers Nikolay Dobrolyubov and Nikolay Chernyshevsky. Chernyshevsky's dissertation *Esteticheskiye otnosheniya iskusstva k deystvitelnosti* (1855; "The Aesthetic Relations of Art to Reality"), the main thesis of which was that art must not only reflect reality but also explain and judge it, provided a starting point for contemporary artists.

From the last third of the 19th century onward, the history of Russian art is the history of a series of school struggles: the Slavophiles against the Westerners; the Academy against the Peredvizhniki ("Wanderers"); and later the joint effort of the last two against a new movement, born in the 1890s and directed by the art review *Mir Iskusstva* ("The World of Art").

The Peredvizhniki was a society formed in 1870 by a group of essentially Romantic artists who, however, regarded themselves as Realists. They seceded from the Academy in 1863 in protest against alien dogmatic formulas and the constricting programs of the Academy's annual competitions. Most prominent among the Peredvizhniki were Ivan Kramskoy, Ilya Repin, Vasily Ivanovich Surikov, Vasily Perov, and Vasily Vereshchagin. The society attached far more importance to the moral and literary aspects of art than to aesthetics. Its artistic creed was realism, national feeling, and social consciousness. Art was to be placed at the service of humanitarian and social ideals; it was to be brought to the people. Accordingly the society organized mobile (*peredvizheniye*) exhibitions—hence the name. The influence of the Peredvizhniki was dominant throughout Russia for nearly 30 years, but by the end of the century it had greatly declined.

CHAPTER SEVEN

PAINTING IN MODERN ART

The phrase "Modern art" has come to denote the innovating and even revolutionary developments in Western painting and the other visual arts since the second half of the 19th century. It embraces a wide variety of movements, styles, theories, and attitudes, the modernity of which resides in a common tendency to repudiate past conventions and precedents in subject matter, mode of depiction, and painting technique alike. Not all the painting of this period has made such a departure; representational work, for example, has continued to appear, particularly in connection with official exhibiting societies. Nevertheless, the idea that some current types of painting are more properly of their time than are others, and for that reason are more interesting or important, applies with particular force to the painting of the last 150 years.

By the mid-19th century, painting was no longer basically in service to either the church or the court but rather was patronized by the upper and middle classes of an increasingly materialistic and secularized Western society. This society was undergoing rapid change because of the growth of science and technology, industrialization, urbanization, and the fundamental questioning of received religious dogmas. Painters were thus confronted with the need to reject traditional, historical, or academic forms and conventions in an effort to create an art that would better reflect the changed social, material, and intellectual conditions of emerging modern life.

Another important, if indirect, stimulus to change was the invention (c. 1839) and advancement of photography and other photomechanical techniques, which freed (or deprived) painting and drawing of their hitherto cardinal roles as the only available means of accurately depicting the visual world. These manually executed arts were thus no longer obliged to serve as the means of recording and disseminating information as they once had been and were eventually freed to explore aesthetically the basic visual elements of line, colour, tone, and composition in a nonrepresentational context. Indeed, an important trend in Modern painting has been that of abstraction—painting in which little or no attempt is made to accurately depict the appearance or form of objects in the realm of nature or the existing physical world. The door of the objective world was thus closed, but the inner world of the imagination offered seemingly infinite possibilities for exploration, as did the manipulation of pigments on a flat surface for their purely intrinsic visual or aesthetic appeal.

The beginnings of Modern painting cannot be clearly demarcated, but it is generally agreed that it started in mid-19th-century France. At the end of that century a succession of varied styles and movements began to arise that are the core of Modern painting and are also one of the high points of the history of the Western visual arts in general.

ORIGINS IN THE 19TH CENTURY

The first appearance of the phrase "Modern art" in the form of a book title was in 1883, when it was used by the French writer Joris-Karl Huysmans to describe the theme of various reviews of painters' work he had collected. Other books on the subject followed, such as the Anglo-Irish novelist George Moore's *Modern Painting* (1893). It was about this time that the term "avant-garde" was introduced by the critic Théodore Duret, who used it to describe certain young painters. From then on, modernity was to be a recurrent concern of artists and critics.

Public acceptance of the new standpoint was slow, however. The first museums dedicated specifically to Modern art grew out of the fervour of individual collectors. The Museum of Modern Art in New York City, the outstanding public collection in the field, was founded in 1929, and the Western capital that today lacks a museum explicitly devoted to Modern art is rare.

The conflict between the new forces and the established academic tradition in France came into the open in 1863. The jury of the Salon, the official exhibition of art sponsored by the French government, rejected more than 4,000 canvases—an unusually high figure. The resulting outcry prompted the emperor Napoleon III to order that the rejected works, if the painters agreed, be shown in a special exhibition known as the Salon des Refusés. The exhibition included works by Édouard Manet, Paul Cézanne, and others. One of the greatest scandals was caused by Manet's painting *The Luncheon on the Grass* (Louvre), which was considered an affront to decency as well as taste. The younger painters became aware of their common aims. Claude Monet had met Pierre-Auguste Renoir, Alfred Sisley, and Jean-Frédéric Bazille studying in the studio of Charles Gleyre. Abandoning academic study, they worked together outdoors in the forest of Fontainebleau, where contacts with some of the Barbizon painters strengthened their direction.

Though the figurative aims of Impressionism can be regarded as the conclusion of 19th-century Realism, the method, which made no attempt to hide even the most basic means of preparing a finished painting, was an original one. Brushstrokes did not pretend to be anything but dashes of paint, thus conveying their coloured message without any disguise or effect at individual illusion. It was in this respect and in the all-embracing unity of colour and handling that resulted, rather than its realism, that Impressionism founded Modern painting.

IMPRESSIONISM

The first steps toward a systematic Impressionist style were taken in France in Monet's coast scenes from 1866 onward. The decisive development took place in 1869, when Monet and Renoir painted together at the resort of La Grenouillère on the Seine River. The resulting pictures suggest that Monet contributed the pattern of separate brushstrokes, the light tonality, and the brilliance of colour; Renoir the overall iridescence, feathery lightness of touch, and delight in the recreation of ordinary people. Working at Louveciennes from 1869, Camille Pissarro evolved the drier and more flexible handling of crumbly paint that was also to be a common feature of Impressionist painting.

It was in the environs of Paris after the Franco-Prussian War that there developed the fully formed landscape style that remains the most popular achievement of Modern painting. An exhibition held in the studio of the photographer Nadar (Gaspard-Félix Tournachon) in 1874 included Monet's picture *Impression: Sunrise*, and it was this work that, by being disparaged as mere "impressionism," gave a name to an entire movement. The exhibition itself revealed three main trends. The Parisian circle around Monet and Renoir had developed the evanescent and sketchlike style the furthest. The vision of those working near Pissarro in Pontoise and Auvers was in general more solid, being firmly rooted in country scenes. A relatively urbane, genrelike trend was detectable in Edgar Degas's picture of Paul Valpinçon and his family at the races called *Carriage at the Races* (1870–73) and Berthe Morisot's *The Cradle* (1873). Manet himself was absent, hoping for academic success; his *Gare Saint-Lazare* (1873), influenced by the Impressionist palette, was accepted at the Salon. Modeling himself on Pissarro, Cézanne sublimated the turbulent emotions of his earlier work in pictures that were studied directly and closely from nature; he followed the method for the rest of his life.

The experiment of an independent exhibition was repeated in 1876, though with fewer participants. In 1877 only 18 artists exhibited. The major painters began to go their separate ways, particularly as there were disputes about whether to continue with the independent exhibitions. Cézanne, who did not exhibit with the Impressionists again, was perhaps the first to realize that a critical stage had been reached. For the first time, a style had been based on the openly individual character of a technique rather than on the form of a particular subject or the way it was formulated. A style that admits to painting as being only a matter of paint raises in a peculiarly acute form the question of how far the qualities of art are intrinsic. Impressionism in the 1870s was inseparable from heightened visual experience of a sensuously satisfying world. But the blocklike shapes in Cézanne's pictures suggest that for him the relationship between the colour

Louis Guillaume, oil on canvas by Paul Cézanne, *c.* 1882; in the Chester Dale Collection, National Gallery of Art, Washington, D.C.

patches on his canvas was equally important. In the years that followed, he systematized his technique into patterns of parallel brushstrokes that gave a new significance to the pictorial surface. An unassuming series of still lifes and self-portraits by Cézanne were painted in 1879–80, and these, when they became known, profoundly impressed the younger generation.

The style of the 1870s was formless from a traditional standpoint. At the beginning of the next decade, Renoir decided that he had gone to the limit with Impressionism, and following a trip to Italy, he set about acquiring a wiry, linear style that was the direct opposite of his relaxed, freely brushed manner of earlier years.

The appearance of a new generation posed a fresh challenge. Georges Seurat was moving away from the empirical standpoint of Impressionism toward a technique (Pointillism) and a form that were increasingly deliberately designed. Paul Gauguin, taking his starting point from Cézanne's style of about 1880, passed from a capricious personal type of Impressionism to a greater use of symbols. He exhibited with the Impressionists from 1880 onward, but it was soon evident that group shows could no longer accommodate the growing diversity. In 1884, after the Salon jury had been particularly harsh, the Société des Artistes Indépendants was formed. The last Impressionist group show was held in 1886. Only Monet and Armand Guillaumin, to whose efforts the group owed much of its eventual recognition, were now in the strict sense Impressionists. Monet continued to build on the original foundation of the style, the rendering of visual impression through colour in paintings that studied a single motif in varying lights. For him the formlessness and the homogeneity of Impressionism were its ultimate virtues.

Impressionism, in one aspect, continued the main direction of 19th-century painting, and after 1880 the movement was an international one, taking on independent national characteristics. In France Impressionism provided a basis for the styles that followed.

SYMBOLISM

During the decades before 1900, the Symbolists were the avant-garde, and one of quite a new kind, influencing not only the arts but also the thought and spirit of the epoch. Maurice Denis, their theoretician, enunciated in 1890 the most famous of their artistic principles:

Remember that a picture—before being a war-horse, a nude or an anecdote of some sort—is essentially a flat surface covered with colours assembled in a certain order.

Such ideas inspired a group of young painters, among whom was Denis himself, to call themselves Nabis (from the Hebrew word for "prophet"). They were in revolt against the faithfulness to nature of Impressionism; in addition they regarded choice of subject as important. They included Paul Ranson, who gave the style a decorative and linear inflection; Pierre Bonnard; and Édouard Vuillard.

Other than the Nabis, one of the chief Symbolists was Odilon Redon, who moved from the same starting point as the Impressionists— the landscape style of the Barbizon school— but in precisely the opposite direction. Redon's visionary charcoal drawings (which he called his black pictures) led to successive series of lithographs that explored the evocative, irrational, and fantastic orders of creation that Impressionism excluded. Redon later wrote:

Nothing in art can be done by will alone. Everything is done by docile submission to the coming of the unconscious . . . for every act of creation, the unconscious sets us a different problem.

Redon established one of the characteristic standpoints of Modern art, and his influence on the younger Symbolists was profound. In 1888 Gauguin settled at Pont-Aven in Brittany. The influential style he developed there was based on the juxtaposition of flat areas of colours enclosed by black contours, the total effect suggesting cloisonné enamel, hence the name Cloisonnisme used to describe this style. The spirit in which Gauguin rendered Breton scenes was mystical. At Pont-Aven, Gauguin was joined by other painters who had begun to work in a similar way. The liberation of Synthetism, as the new style was called, indeed worked like a charm, and after the Café Volpini exhibition of 1889 it spread rapidly. The movement was linked with literature and, in particular, with drama.

The decorative style known as Art Nouveau, or Jugendstil, spread across Europe and the Americas in the 1890s. The pursuit of natural and organic sources for form still further alienated art from the descriptive purpose that had been the basis of figurative style, and an artistic movement without taint of historicism that molded the fine arts, architecture, and craftsmanship in a single, consistent taste recovered the creative unity that had been lost since the early 18th century.

THE END OF THE 19TH-CENTURY TRADITION

Until Seurat no painter had expressly founded a style on the intrinsic reactions of colour to colour and a codified vocabulary of expressive forms. The consistent granulation of colour in Seurat's work from 1885 onward was specific to the picture, not to the sensation or the subject. The coherent images of space and light that he made out of this granulation ended with him. Seurat's followers, grouped as Neo-Impressionists, developed his technique rather than his vision. Seurat's influence was nonetheless widespread and fertile; his system in itself supplied a clarity that painters needed.

Starry Night over the Rhône, oil on canvas by Vincent van Gogh, 1888; in the Musée D'Orsay, Paris

It was Neo-Impressionism that was in the ascendant when the Dutch painter Vincent van Gogh arrived in Paris in 1886. The emotional travail evident in van Gogh's early work was marvelously lightened in the new aesthetic climate. But in his hands the dashes of pure colour turned and twisted, trading invisible and unstable lines of force. They were woven into rhythmical and convulsive patterns reflecting the mounting intensity of his own feelings. Such patterns converted the Neo-Impressionist style into something quite different—a forerunner of what was to be known as Expressionism. Other painters were less radical in their approach.

In the meantime, the older Impressionists were producing the broadly conceived works that crowned their artistic achievement and formed, as it seems in retrospect, the great traditional masterpieces of Modern art. The end of the 19th century came to be defined by a style known as the fin de siècle (French: "end of the century"), an artistic climate of sophistication, escapism, extreme aestheticism, world-weariness, and fashionable despair.

THE 20TH CENTURY

By 1903 the impetus of Symbolism was expended and a new and enigmatic mood was forming. The new attitude drew on a vein that was comic, poetic, and fantastic, exploring an irrational quality akin to humour inherent in the creative process itself, as well as on a reserve of ironic detachment. The new painters drew strength from unexpected sources. The work of Henri Rousseau, who had exhibited at the Indépendants since 1886, attracted attention. The apparent innocence of his pictures gave them a kind of imaginative grandeur that seemed beyond the reach of any art founded on sophistication.

The art of supposedly primitive peoples had a special appeal in the early years of the 20th century. Gauguin, who had made direct contact with it in his last years, proved prophetic not only in the forms he adopted but in the spirit of his approach. Maurice de Vlaminck and André Derain, who met in 1900, evolved a style together based on crude statements of strong colours. Henri Matisse had been moving more circumspectly in the same direction. The apparent ferocity of the works that the three exhibited in 1905 earned them the nickname of the Fauves ("Wild Beasts"). It appears that Matisse was responsible for introducing Pablo Picasso to African sculpture. Picasso had already shown signs of dissatisfaction with existing canons; his use of fin de siècle styles in his earliest works has a quality close to irony. Primitive art, both African and Iberian, provided him with an austerity and detachment that led after 1906 to a radical metamorphosis of the image and style hitherto habitual in European art. In 1904 Ernst Ludwig Kirchner, at Dresden, discovered the art of the Pacific Islands as well as African art. His first reflection of the primitive spirit was parallel to that of the Fauves and may have depended on them, if only partially.

The idea of art, first and last, as a matter of expression (in contrast to Impressionism) was common to Germany and France in the first decade of the 20th century. In *Notes of a Painter* (1908), Matisse hardly differentiates expression from decoration; his ideal of art as "something like a good armchair in which to rest" explicitly excluded the distortion and disquiet that earned the style of Kirchner and Die Brücke ("The Bridge") group, which was founded in 1905, the label of Expressionism.

The transformation of painting after 1907 was particularly apparent in works executed in Germany. The earliest mature works of Wassily Kandinsky, who had come to Munich from Moscow in 1896, were painted in a jewellike, fairy-tale Cloisonniste style. His first nonfigurative watercolour was painted in 1910, and in the same year he wrote much of *Concerning the Spiritual in Art*, which converted the aesthetic doctrines of Goethe to the purposes of the new art. The series of "Improvisations" that followed preserved reminiscences of figuration, made illegible by the looseness of the pictorial structure; their diffuse and amorphous consistency had little connection with the main objectives of painting at the time. In the first decade of the 20th century, the idea of painting implied by Post-Impressionism and that of a reasoned structure analogous to the structure of nature, if not to appearances, were far from exhausted. The influence of Kandinsky's "Improvisations" from 1911 onward, though delayed, was nonetheless great and pointed in a direction that abstract painting was to take 40 years later.

The Munich group Der Blaue Reiter ("The Blue Rider"), named after one of Kandinsky's earlier pictures, was formed in 1911 to represent the new tendencies when Kandinsky and Franz Marc withdrew from the heterogeneous Neue Künstlervereinigung ("New Artists' Association"). The group soon became, in its turn, a broadly based assembly of the international avant-garde artists of the day. Among the early members of the group, the Russian Alexey von Jawlensky evolved a structured form of Expressionism that culminated in the 1930s in a series of abstractions of a head, but the chief importance of the group was as a stage in the development of the Swiss painter Paul Klee.

CUBISM AND ITS CONSEQUENCES

Picasso's "Primitivism," as it came to be called, culminated in 1907 in the enigmatic and famous picture *Les Demoiselles d'Avignon.*

Those who saw it were astonished and perplexed, not only by an arbitrary disruption in the right-hand part of the picture of the continuity that had always united an image but also by the defiant unloveliness, which made it plain that the traditional beauties of art, the appeal of the subject, and the credibility of its imitation were now, at any rate to Picasso, finally irrelevant. Reactions were mixed, but its effect on his associates was profound. Matisse and Georges Braque, who, unlike Picasso, had been experimenting with Fauvism, immediately started painting female nudes of similar stridency. Subsequently, however, Matisse turned back toward relatively traditional forms and the flooding colour that chiefly concerned him. Braque, on the other hand, became more and more closely associated with Picasso, and Cubism, as the new style was labeled by one of Braque's hostile critics in the following year, was the result of their collaboration.

In the first phase, lasting into 1909, the focus of their work was the accentuation and disruption of planes. In the second phase, from 1910 to 1912, the irrelevance of the subject, in any integral form, became evident. It was no longer necessary to travel in search of a motif; any still life would do as well. The essence of the picture was in the treatment. The great Cubist pictures were meditations on the intrinsic character of the

detached Cézannesque facets and contours,
out of which the almost-illegible images
were built. Indeed, the objects were not so
much depicted as denoted by linear signs, a
spiral for the scrolled head of a violin or the
trademark from a label for a bottle, which
were superimposed on the shifting, half-
contradictory flux of shapes. The element of
paradox is essential; even when it approaches
monumental grandeur, Cubism has a
quality that eludes solemn exposition. Subtle
and elegant geometric puns build up into
massive demonstrations of pictorial structure,
demonstrations that its complex parallels
and conjunctions build nothing so firmly and
so memorably as the picture itself. This proof
that figurative art creates an independent
reality is the central proposition of modern art,
and it has had a profound effect not only on
painting and sculpture, as well as on the arts
of design that depend on them, but also on
the intellectual climate of the age.

The experimental investigation of what
reality meant in artistic terms then took a
daring turn that was unparalleled since
pictorial illusion had been isolated five
centuries earlier. The Cubists proceeded
to embody real material from the actual
world within the picture. They included first
stenciled lettering, then pasted paper, and
later solid objects; the reality of art as they
saw it absorbed them all. This assemblage of

material, called collage, led in 1912 to the third phase of the movement, Synthetic Cubism, which continued until 1914. The textured and patterned planes were composed into forms more like pictorial objects in themselves than recognizable figurations. In the later work of Picasso and Braque, it is again possible to construe their pictorial code as referring plainly to the objective world. The message of Cubism remained clear: meaning had been shown to reside in the structure of the style, the basic geometry implied in the Post-Impressionist handling of life. The message spread rapidly.

The first theoretical work on the movement, *On Cubism*, by the French painters Albert Gleizes and Jean Metzinger, was published in 1912. It was argued that geometric and mathematical principles of general validity could be deduced from the style. An exhibition in the same year, called Section d'Or ("Golden Section"), represented all Cubism's adherents except the two creators. Cubism stimulated parallel tendencies in The Netherlands, Italy, and Russia. In The Netherlands, Piet Mondrian, on the basis of Cézanne and the Dutch painters of the fin de siècle, had reached a very simple, symbolic style analogous to the Dutch landscape. He first saw Cubist paintings in 1910 and moved to Paris two years later. The subsequent resolution of his sense of natural conflict into increasingly bare rectangular designs balancing vertical against horizontal and white against areas of primary colour is one of the achievements of Modern art. In 1917 the de Stijl movement formed in The Netherlands around him, with lasting consequences for the architecture, design, and typography of the century.

In Italy in 1909 the poet Filippo Marinetti issued a program for all the arts under the name of Futurism. He rejected the art of the past and exalted energy, strength, movement, and the power of the modern machine. In painting, his ideas were taken up by such artists as Carlo Carrà. Umberto Boccioni, and Giacomo Balla. They reveal that, under its vivid fragmentation, the vision of Futurism was not far from the photographic. Its imperative mood and disruptive tactics nonetheless had their effect, finding an echo in Britain in Wyndham Lewis's Vorticist circle, which sought to relate art and literature to the industrial process.

In Russia, where Western developments were well known, the avant-garde, with its own roots in primitive art, had already evolved a simplified Expressionistic style. Kazimir Malevich produced formalized images of peasants at work that anticipated the later style of Fernand Léger. The striplike and often abstract formulations of Mikhail Larionov and Natalya Gontcharova, to which they gave the name of Rayonism, date from 1911. In 1912 Malevich exhibited his first "Cubo-Futurist" works, in which the figures were reduced to dynamic coloured blocks, and in 1913 he followed these with a

Eiffel Tower, oil on canvas by Robert Delaunay, 1910–11; in the Art Institute of Chicago

black square on a white background. This increasing tendency to abstraction reached its culmination in 1915 with the arrival of what he called Suprematism, in which simple geometric elements provided the whole dynamic force. The Russian movement, complicated by its own politics, was both accelerated and eventually broken by the Revolution, which gave it, for a time, a social function that the avant-garde has hardly achieved elsewhere. The Russian artists dispersed after 1922, however, and their legacy, the tradition of Constructivism, was transmitted to western Europe.

Prismatic colour, the element in Cézanne that the Cubists had neglected in dismantling his style, was taken up by Robert Delaunay. Delaunay's variety of Cubism was named Orphism, after Orpheus, the poet and musician of ancient Greek myth. The essential discovery of Orphism was proclaimed as a realization that "colour is both form and subject." After an exquisite series of "Windows," Delaunay freed himself from representation and based his designs on the effects of simultaneous colour contrast. Delaunay realized that a new order of painting was beginning, but his immediate influence was strongest abroad.

FANTASY AND THE IRRATIONAL

The identity of a work of art as a thing in itself, independent of representation, was on the way to general recognition when the outbreak of war in 1914 interrupted artistic life throughout most of Europe. The activities of a group of painters, writers, and musicians who sought refuge in Zürich reflected the disorientation and disillusion of the time. Dada, as the movement was called, owed much to the iconoclasm of the Cubists and to the polemical tactics of the Futurists. Nonetheless its attack on art was fundamentally artistic; one wing of the avant-garde has owed allegiance to the Dadaist tradition ever since. As well as the need continually to attack the limits of the fine arts, it was felt important to "épater ["shock"] les bourgeois."

The Dadaists enlarged the field open to artists in three ways. They questioned the idea that some subjects were simply not relevant to painting, a question that had been hovering over art for some time, by the simple expedient of arguing that anything and everything was fair game. The repetitive and amorphous trends of Impressionism had in fact already given grounds for such a supposition. The next step was to make a reluctant public accept that any object was a work of art if an artist chose to proclaim it one. In 1914 Marcel Duchamp, the exhibitor of serial images of movement in the Section d'Or, produced a bottle rack bought in a Paris store. Better and more épatant still, he submitted a urinal to a New York exhibition under a pseudonym in 1917. Duchamp did not paint again, and this is perhaps the single Dadaist gesture that time has failed to reconcile with art. It was also the Dadaists who posed the question, if art (as Redon had realized) is not within the reach of will, how is it different from chance? Jean Arp made collages and then reliefs from random shapes obtained "according to the laws of chance." Of all modern artists, he examined most closely the side of art akin to humour. Similarly, the Dadaists explored such elements as incongruity and dissociation, a process that led the way to Surrealism. Finally and almost incidentally, they asked, if the presentation of movement is proper to art, why not movement itself? Viking Eggeling and Hans Richter, with animated drawings and film, made the first works in a kinetic tradition that even by the late 1980s showed no sign of abating.

The painter who, more than any other, focused on incongruity—a feature that in painting involves the reinstatement of the subject, rather than its treatment, at the centre of art—was Giorgio De Chirico, an Italian born in Greece. De Chirico, rooted in the Mediterranean world, created from 1910 onward unforgettable images of its dereliction. In the immediate postwar years, he pioneered a style of emblematic, half-abstract still life called *pittura metafisica* ("metaphysical painting"), but by 1924, when the Surrealists began to work a similar vein of fantasy, De Chirico had changed; and in later life he disavowed his early achievement. Metaphysical painting had one unexpected sequel, the serene realism of Giorgio Morandi. Meanwhile, Kurt Schwitters in Germany developed the mediums of collage and assemblage in the new spirit. Francis Picabia, who was associated with Duchamp in the United States during the war, joined forces with the Swiss Dadaists in 1918; his contribution was an epigrammatic elegance of style. The German Max Ernst was the most resourceful pictorial technician of the movement and a continually fertile inventor.

It was in 1917 that the term "Surrealism" was coined, when the poet Guillaume Apollinaire described the style of the ballet *Parade*, for which Picasso had painted the sets, as:

> ... *a sort of surrealism in which I see a point of departure for a series of manifestations of that New Spirit which ... promises to transform arts and manners from top to bottom with universal joy.*

The manifesto of the Surrealist movement, which was composed by the poet André Breton, did not appear until 1924, however. Surrealism meant different things in different people's hands, but a common feature was absorption in the fantastic and irrational. The questions posed by Dada also preoccupied Surrealists, but for them the problem of the involuntary, fortuitous element in art, for example, was clearly open to psychological solution. The Surrealists demanded "pure psychic automatism"; the automatic drawings that the French artist André Masson made from 1925 onward and, on a more mechanical level, the frottage ("rubbing") devices of Ernst, which added to painting the evocative effect of fortuitously dappled textures, introduced an element that flourished even more fully 20 years later. Another discovery made in the wake of Dada was similarly delayed in its full impact: *Parade* had been the culmination of a series of musical compositions by Erik Satie that were based on ironic quotations of popular material. In the early 1920s the Americans

Stuart Davis and Man Ray made paintings out of the designs on commercial packaging, foreshadowing the Pop Art of the 1950s.

The greatest achievement of Surrealist painting, however, was the invention of a new genre: fantastic realism—the prosaic, quasi-photographic rendering of the forms of fantasy and dream. The invention was the work, after De Chirico, of the Frenchman Yves Tanguy and the Spaniard Salvador Dalí. In the pictorial world of Dalí, everyday things undergo a transformation

Several works by Salvador Dalí on display in the Dalí Theatre-Museum in Figueres, Spain

that can be almost disturbing; in that of Tanguy, forms are more suggestive than related to actual objects. A different aspect of this dream realism, one that is particularly disturbing, was shown by the Belgian René Magritte.

In the years after 1918, a mood of classical consolidation affected some painters. In Germany a "New Objectivity" (Die Neue Sachlichkeit) was imposed on Expressionism; the eventual synthesis appeared in the brutal paintings of Max Beckmann. In France the Italian-born Amedeo Modigliani, affected by the simplicity of the Romanian-born sculptor Constantin Brancusi, arrived at a delicate linear realism, the last of the great Post-Impressionist styles.

The Expressionist tradition was developed to an extreme of agonized distortion by Chaim Soutine. Another Russian-born member of the school of Paris, Marc Chagall, who had been influenced both by Cubism and the Russian avant-garde, discovered in the 1920s an individual and inconsequent vein of pictorial fancy. The sombre and devotional art of the Frenchman Georges Rouault bore the marks of his training with Gustave Moreau and as a stained-glass maker. Its crude force had been developed in the context of Fauvism, but the vision was one of refined introspection. The vigour and freedom of Fauvism was developed in the opposite direction in the decorative, extrovert style of another French painter, Raoul

Dufy. The classicizing trend of the 1920s had a remarkable sequel in the work of the mural painters of Mexico. One such, Diego Rivera, had learned the formal lessons of Cubism in Paris; José Clemente Orozco was more dependent on the folk art of his country. Their frescoes combined grandeur with a legibility and social awareness rare in Modern art.

The greatest imaginative achievements between World Wars I and II were, however, again those of Picasso. In the years immediately following World War I he had painted a series of solidly modeled yet oddly ironic figure pictures. Then his mood changed, and in 1925 *The Three Dancers* reintroduced an anarchic and convulsive quality. The ambiguities and transformations of his art, both in painting and sculpture, have an emotional character that is entirely his own, but the enlargement of the artistic language greatly influenced others. The metamorphosis of natural shape into abstracted forms that nevertheless curve and bulge with their own life, a metamorphosis initiated by Picasso, became the international style of the early 1930s.

The development of abstract painting between the wars was comparatively slow. Klee (in 1921) and Kandinsky (in 1922) gravitated to the Bauhaus, the school in Germany whose work at Weimar and later at Dessau deeply influenced architecture and design as well as basic teaching. Kandinsky was concerned with refining the geometric ingredient of his work. Klee developed the poetic and fantastic elements of his art with an inconsequent fertility. The systematic purity of the Bauhaus approach survived longest in the work of Josef Albers, who moved to the United States in 1933. In 1940 Mondrian moved to New York City, and his last dynamic pictures reflect the new environment. Mondrian's work was appreciated by only a small circle. In the 1930s some paintings were executed by artists who formed themselves into groups, such as Abstraction-Création in Paris, Unit One in London, and the Association of American Abstract Artists in New York City. The work of these groups attained wider recognition only after World War II.

AFTER 1945

In the postwar period, the Expressionist tradition was revived in the new spirit by the "Cobra" group of painters from Copenhagen, Brussels, and Amsterdam who came together in Paris in 1948. Surrealism also proved remarkably durable. Among its adherents, the American Joseph Cornell had been evolving from the techniques of collage and assemblage a personal and evocative form of image; Polish artist Hans Bellmer and the German Richard Lindner, working in Paris and New York, respectively, explored private and obsessive themes; they were recognized as among the most individual talents of their generation. In general, the most idiosyncratic and anarchic qualities of art were being developed as a new tradition, while geometric abstraction was seen to be the natural basis for the arts that are public and communal in purpose.

The presence of a number of the pioneer Surrealists in the United States during World War II affected later developments there. Surrealism's element of psychic automatism, particularly the spontaneous calligraphy of Masson, was particularly influential. The possibilities had, in fact, been implicit in Modern painting for at least two decades; in Paris in the 1920s, Jean Fautrier was already basing pictures on spontaneous and informal gestures with paint. In the United States in the 1940s, however, fresh impetus came from the impulsive play of colour in the work of the influential teacher Hans Hofmann. The movement that became known as Abstract Expressionism represented a decisive departure from its European sources, not only because the homogeneous consistency of a painted surface in itself took on a new meaning in the expansive U.S. conditions but at least equally because of the exceptional personality of Jackson Pollock. The style Pollock adopted in 1947 reflected an original involvement in the act of painting that transcended deliberation or control.

In contrast to Pollock's work, paintings executed by Willem de Kooning at the time, though equally sweeping and ungovernable, showed a recurrent figurative reference. Another Abstract Expressionist, Franz Kline, claimed, in executing his shapes like huge black and white ideograms, to be in some sense depicting figurative images. Critic Harold Rosenberg dubbed the group "action painters." In the course of the 1950s their influence was felt in almost every country. The climate of artistic opinion that spread outward from New York made possible flamboyant gesture paintings such as those of the French-born Georges Mathieu.

The idea of painting as a homogeneous allover fabric led at the same time to other quite separate developments. Prompted by the primitive and psychotic imagery that he called *l'art brut* ("raw art"), Jean Dubuffet embarked on an extraordinarily resourceful series of experiments in translating the raw material of the world into pictures. The energy that fills the works of the American painter Mark Tobey is by comparison gentle and lyrical and much influenced by East Asian art. Dubuffet's example inspired the abstract "matter" painting that developed in several countries around 1950. At its best, as in the work of the Catalan Antonio

Tapies, this style conveys a strong sense of natural substance.

NEW FORMS

In painting, generally, a new directness was strikingly combined with a new simplicity. In the five years before his death in 1954, Matisse made a series of large *gouaches découpées* in which the increasingly abstract images were created solely by the juxtaposition of sharply cut patches of brilliant colour. Their influence was widespread and by no means confined to painters. Even from other starting points, painters were reaching similar conclusions. The very simple yet resonant colour combinations of the New York painter Mark Rothko or the grand severity of another American, Barnett Newman, furnish examples.

Abstract painting was revealing far wider potentialities than had been apparent between World Wars I and II, but figurative styles showed a new freedom as well. The Swiss Alberto Giacometti, who had worked as a Surrealist, evolved his sensation of the visual impact of figures in space. Francis Bacon in Britain uncovered unexpected and startling connotations in the apparition of a human likeness on canvas.

Painting in the 1960s not only sought originality; it took up a deliberately extreme position that may have seemed almost to pass the bounds of art. Paintings might be extremely large. Alternatively, they might be extreme in some other respect, such as the canvases of the Frenchman Yves Klein, which showed only a plain, arresting blue colour, or the black pictures of the American Ad Reinhardt, with variations so slight as to be hardly perceptible. The element of apparent chance in action painting explained the way the stains of colour in the work of the American painter Morris Louis appeared to flow and soak across the canvas as if of their own accord.

The tradition of Dada and its skepticism regarding what had once been the received definition of art prompted continual experiment with the techniques of assemblage. Robert Rauschenberg in the United States sought to place his subtly calculated "combine paintings" (collections of contrasting objects joined to make an ensemble) in the gap between reality and art, contrasting the significance of paint with the borrowed imagery and objects juxtaposed with it. Jasper Johns, Rauschenberg's associate, worked with preexisting designs such as targets and the U.S. flag, giving them an ironic look when subjected to incorporation in his works. In the borrowed imagery and popular quotations, on which much painting was based in the years that followed, the irony was intensified to the point of ceasing to be irony at all. Roy Lichtenstein took strip cartoons and other banal imagery as the motifs for pictures. Another American, Claes Oldenburg, began by reconstructing common things out of the random pictorial substance of Abstract Expressionism; his later reconstructions of the rigid furniture of everyday life are tailored out of limp plastic sheeting.

There is nothing random about the typical art of the 1960s. On the contrary, it was planned exactly and normally carried out by an efficient, almost mechanical-seeming system. Hard-edge painting developed into a wide range of planar styles having in common only their exploitation of optical reactions and the element of shock that is the visual concomitant of sharp contrast. The initial tendency was to exclude sensations from the aesthetic canon, but in the event a whole region of visual meaning, void for uncertainty since abstraction began, was reclaimed for painting. Optical art, or Op Art, emphasizes movement, whether potential, actual, or relative, and such effects have been ingeniously investigated by the Groupe de Recherche d'Art Visuel ("Group for Visual Research"), founded in Paris in 1960, and the Zero group in Düsseldorf, Germany.

Other developments have proved more fertile. In the hands of the American painters Kenneth Noland and Frank Stella, painting discovered new shapes, both within the rectangular canvas and beyond it. The extreme in this reduction of means and sophistication of aesthetics was perhaps reached when a group of sculptors in the United States and England

POP ART

Pop art featured commonplace objects (such as comic strips, soup cans, road signs, and hamburgers) as subject matter and often physically incorporated them in the work. The Pop art movement was largely a British and American cultural phenomenon of the late 1950s and '60s and was named by the art critic Lawrence Alloway in reference to the prosaic iconography of its painting and sculpture. Works by Pop artists such as Roy Lichtenstein, Andy Warhol, and Claes Oldenburg were characterized by their portrayal of any and all aspects of popular culture that had a powerful impact on contemporary life; their iconography—taken from television, comic books, movie magazines, and all forms of advertising—was presented emphatically and objectively, without praise or condemnation but with overwhelming immediacy, and by means of the precise commercial techniques used by the media from which the iconography itself was borrowed.

Pop art represented an attempt to return to a more objective, universally acceptable form of art after the dominance in both the United States and Europe of the highly personal Abstract Expressionism. It was also iconoclastic, rejecting both the supremacy of the "high art" of the past and the pretensions of other contemporary avant-garde art. Pop art became a cultural event because of its close reflection of a particular social situation and because its easily comprehensible images were immediately exploited by the mass media. Although the critics of Pop art described it as vulgar, sensational, nonaesthetic, and a joke, its proponents (a minority in the art world) saw it as an art that was democratic and nondiscriminatory, bringing together both connoisseurs and untrained viewers.

turned to investigate the possibilities of minimal and primary forms, normally the simplest geometric solids, alone or arranged in baldly repetitive series. Here, it is the spectator who brings the interpretation and supplies the art. The proposition had the apparent preposterousness expected of avant-garde art, yet it seemed likely, in its turn, to shed light on problems that are very much older.

It is characteristic of sculpture and painting in the 20th century to deal more and more consciously and directly with the ultimate definition of art. The perennial compulsion to reverse previously accepted definitions has threatened ever more directly the recognizable identity of art. At the end of the 1960s the tendency to emphasize the systems and attitudes of art rather than its product led to a move in several countries to deny the validity of the art object. Instead artists prepared written specifications for ideal, imaginary art, the fulfillment of which was superfluous, or self-sufficient programs for performances paradoxically analogous to some aspect of the more familiar artistic acts. Conceptual art (artwork whose medium is an idea) has opened the way to activities notable in their defiance of conventional expectations.

In the 1970s, critical and public interest centred on the reductive constructions of Minimalism and the nihilistic questioning of conceptual art. The late 1970s and early 1980s, however, saw a resurgence of excitement in painting and a return to figurative representation. A new movement called Neo-Expressionism arose in New York City and in the art capitals of western Europe, especially in Germany, combining the heavy paint surfaces and dynamic brushstrokes of Abstract Expressionism with the emotional tone of early 20th-century German Expressionism. The new movement's subject matter ranged from basically literal, though self-consciously primitive, treatments of the human figure to a range of imaginary subjects indicative of modern urban life, particularly its glamour, alienation, and menace. A notable characteristic of Neo-Expressionism was the newly prominent role played in its commercial acceptance by gallery owners and art dealers who adroitly publicized the

Untitled (Yellow Tar and Feathers), acrylic, oilstick, crayon, paper collage, and feathers on joined wood panels by Jean-Michel Basquiat, 1982. Here it is shown during a November 13, 2013, auction at Sotheby's in New York, at which the work was sold to a private collector.

movement's artists. Indeed, Neo-Expressionism's sudden success was an indication of the growing commercialization of the avant-garde and its unhesitating acceptance by wealthy, influential collectors and progressive-minded museum curators. Some critics voiced doubts over what they saw as the reflexive pursuit of artistic novelty under the influence of commercial pressures, and some even asserted that critical and public acclaim had to some extent become divorced from the goals of finding and patronizing painters whose works had lasting artistic significance.

The painter, who at varying moments in history has been regarded either as an artisan (by the church or government) or as a genius whose individuality and inspiration are without bounds, is a key figure in our understanding of history, culture, and the evolution of the arts. The painter's choice of subject, technique, and material all provide insight into our view of the world and the time period in which each particular artist lived. Paintings also acquire meaning through their continued critique— understanding that "meaning" encompasses the totality of context, content, and significance. Thus, the study of the history of painting is a constant play between understanding the intent and means of the artist—along with his or her particular constraints—and assigning our own interpretation of the work's visual language through the lens of our own time.

In the 21st century the proliferation of images and almost unbridled access to reproductions of paintings from all periods—afforded by the Internet and digital photography—has greatly expanded and shaped our understanding of the history of painting. In recent years, pluralism has come to define the medium, and painters draw from diverse sources of inspiration, techniques, and historical styles—all through a contemporary lens. Given this pluralism it serves the modern critic well to glance back through the various movements and periods in the history of painting to grasp the restless endeavour to extend the boundaries of expression in Western art.

GLOSSARY

aniconic Opposed to the use of idols or images.

automatism Suspension of the conscious mind to release subconscious images.

avant-garde A group of people who develop new and often very surprising ideas in any field, especially in the arts.

bodegón Scene of daily life with strong elements of still life in the composition.

cartoon A design, drawing, or painting made as a model for the finished work.

chiaroscuro The arrangement or treatment of light and dark parts in a pictorial work of art.

classicism The principles or style embodied in the literature, art, or architecture of ancient Greece and Rome.

cloisonné enamel A technique in which metal strips differentiate the colour areas of the design, thereby creating an outline effect.

codex A manuscript book especially of Scripture, classics, or ancient annals.

contrapposto The twisting of a figure so that one half is in opposition to the other.

didacticism Intended primarily to teach rather than to entertain.

ecclesiastical Of or relating to a church.

fin de siècle Of, relating to, or characteristic of the close of the 19th century and especially its literary and artistic climate of sophistication, world-weariness, and fashionable despair.

fresco The art of painting on freshly spread moist lime plaster with water-based pigments.

frieze A sculptured or richly ornamented band (as on a building or piece of furniture).

frottage The technique of creating a design by rubbing (as with a pencil) over an object placed underneath the paper or a composition made by such technique.

funerary Of, used for, or associated with burial.

icon A religious image usually painted on a small wooden panel.

iconoclasm The doctrine, practice, or attitude of destroying religious images or opposing their veneration.

illuminated manuscript A handwritten book decorated with gold or silver, brilliant colours, or elaborate designs or miniature pictures.

impasto The thick application of a pigment to a canvas or panel in painting.

lectionary A book or list of lections, or the liturgical readings for a particular day, for the church year.

metope The space between two triglyphs of a Doric frieze often adorned with carved work.

mysticism The experience of mystical union or direct communication with God.

patronage The support or influence of a patron, or one who gives generous financial support or approval.

plasticity The capacity for being molded or changed in form or shape.

rationalism The belief that reason and experience and not emotions or religious beliefs should be the basis for your actions, opinions, etc.

realism The theory or practice in art, literature, and theater of showing things as they really are and without idealization.

sacra conversazione "Sacred conversation" in Italian; a representation of the Holy Family (Madonna, Christ Child, and a group of saints, angels, or donors) in which the figures seem to be engaged in conversation.

scriptorium A copying room for scribes, especially in a medieval monastery.

slip Liquid clay that covers the pottery body.

BIBLIOGRAPHY

Among the standard surveys of the history of Western art are Fred S. Kleiner, *Gardner's Art Through the Ages*, 14th ed. (2012); Penelope J.E. Davies, H.W. Janson, et. al. *Janson's History of Art*, 8th ed. (2011); and Hugh Honour and John Fleming, *The Visual Arts: A History*, 7th ed. (2013). Among the major standard reference works are the *Encyclopedia of World Art*, 16 vol. (1959–83); *McGraw-Hill Dictionary of Art*, edited by Bernard S. Myers, 5 vol. (1969); Harold Osborne (ed.), *The Oxford Companion to Art* (1970, reprinted 1984); and the *Praeger Encyclopedia of Art*, 5 vol. (1971). See also Arnold Hauser, *The Social History of Art*, trans. from German, 4 vol., 3rd ed. (1999); Elizabeth G. Holt (ed.), *A Documentary History of Art*, 3 vol. (1957–66, vol. 1 and 2 reprinted in 1982); Peter Murray and Linda Murray, *A Dictionary of Art and Artists*, 7th ed. (2013); and E.H. Gombrich, *The Story of Art*, 16th rev. ed. (1995). Later reference works include the *Larousse Dictionary of Painters* (1981; originally published in French, 1976); and David Piper (ed.), *The Random House Library of Painting and Sculpture*, 4 vol. (1981). F. David Martin, *Sculpture and Enlivened Space: Aesthetics and History* (1981), examines the comparative importance of painting and sculpture in Western art.

EUROPEAN METAL AGE CULTURES

Stuart Piggott, *Ancient Europe, from the Beginnings of Agriculture to Classical Antiquity* (1965); and Walter Torbrugge, *Prehistoric European Art* (1968; originally published in German, 1968), provide general surveys. There is a vast literature on the Aegean and eastern Mediterranean, including Spyridon Marinatos, *Crete and Mycenae* (1960; originally published in Greek, 1959), photographs by Max Hirmer; Reynold Higgins, *Minoan and Mycenaean Art*, rev. ed. (1981); and Spyridon Marinatos, "Life and Art in Prehistoric Thera," *Proceedings of the British Academy*, vol. 57 (1972). Sir Arthur Evans, *The Palace of Minos: A Comparative Account of the Successive Stages of the Early Cretan Civilization as Illustrated by the Discoveries at Knossos*, 4 vol. in 6 (1921–35, reissued 1964), is a classic work but is superseded in part by Richard W. Hutchinson, *Prehistoric Crete* (1962, reprinted 1968); Sinclair Hood, *The Minoans: The Story of Bronze Age Crete* (1971); and Keith Branigan, *The Foundations of Palatial Crete* (1970). For Helladic art, the best works are George E. Mylonas, *Mycenae and the Mycenaean Age* (1966); and Lord William Taylour, *The Mycenaeans*, rev. ed. (1983). For Cyprus, see Vassos Karageorghis, *Cyprus*

(1969), with a useful bibliography. Among the numerous works on the western Mediterranean are the following: Antonio Arribas, *The Iberians* (1964); L. Bernabò Brea, *Sicily Before the Greeks* (rev. ed., 1966; originally published in Italian, 1966); David H. Trump, *Central and Southern Italy Before Rome* (1966); David Randall-MacIver, *The Iron Age in Italy: A Study of Those Aspects of the Early Civilization Which Are neither Villanovan nor Etruscan* (1927, reprinted 1974) and *Villanovans and Early Etruscans: A Study of the Early Iron Age in Italy as It Is Seen near Bologna, in Etruria and in Latium* (1924); Mario Moretti and Guglielmo Maetzke, *The Art of the Etruscans* (1970; originally published in Italian, 1969); P.J. Riis, *An Introduction to Etruscan Art* (1953; originally published in Danish, 1948); Raymond Bloch, *The Etruscans* (1958; originally published in French, 1958); Massimo Pallotino, *Etruscan Painting*, trans. from French (1952), and *Art of the Etruscans*, trans. from French (1955); Margaret Guido, *Sardinia* (1964); and John D. Evans, *Malta* (1959). For northern European art, see Paul Jacobsthal, *Early Celtic Art*, 2 vol. (1944, reprinted 1970). See also John E. Pfeiffer, *The Creative Explosion: An Inquiry into the Origins of Art and Religion* (1982); André Leroi-Gourhan, *The Dawn of European Art: An Introduction to Palaeolithic Cave Painting*

(1982; originally published in Italian, 1981); and Pierre Amiet et al., *Art in the Ancient World: A Handbook of Styles and Forms*, trans. from French (1981).

ANCIENT GREEK

Important general works include John D. Beazley and Bernard Ashmole, *Greek Sculpture and Painting to the End of the Hellenistic Period* (1932, reprinted 1966); John Boardman, *Greek Art*, new rev. ed. (1985); John Boardman et al., *Greek Art and Architecture* (1967; originally published in German, 1966), with photographs by Max Hirmer; Rhys Carpenter, *The Esthetic Basis of Greek Art of the Fifth and Fourth Centuries B.C.*, rev. ed. (1959); Gisella Richter, *A Handbook of Greek Art*, 8th ed. (1983), and *Archaic Greek Art Against Its Historical Background* (1949); George Boas (ed.), *The Greek Tradition* (1939), a collection of essays published in connection with an exhibition and accompanied by its catalog, George Boas et al., *The Greek Tradition in Painting and the Minor Arts* (1939); Bernhard Schweitzer, *Greek Geometric Art* (1971; originally published in German, 1969); and Vincent J. Bruno, *Form and Color in Greek Painting* (1977). Among the standard studies on vase painting are Paolo E. Arias, *A History of 1000 Years of Greek Vase Painting* (1962; originally published in Italian, 1960), with photographs by Max Hirmer; John D. Beazley, *The Development of Attic Black-Figure* (1951, reprinted 1986), *Potter and Painter in Ancient Athens* (1944), *Attic Black-Figure Vase-Painters* (1956, reprinted 1978), and *Attic Red-Figure Vase-Painters*, 2nd ed., 3 vol. (1963, reissued 1984); Ernst Buschor, *Greek Vase Painting* (1921, reprinted 1971; originally published in German, 1913); Joseph V. Noble, *The Techniques of Painted Attic Pottery* (1965); and Martin Robertson, *Greek Painting* (1959; reissued 1979). See also Manolis Andronikos, *Vergina: The Royal Tombs and the Ancient City* (1984; originally published in Greek, 1984). Martin Robertson, *A Shorter History of Greek Art* (1981), is an excellent condensed study of Greek art from the Geometric through the Hellenistic periods.

ROMAN

General surveys include George M.A. Hanfmann, *Roman Art: A Modern Survey of the Art of Imperial Rome* (1964, reissued 1975); Heinz Kähler, *The Art of Rome and Her Empire* (1963; originally published in German, 1962);

German Hafner, *Art of Rome, Etruria, and Magna Graecia*, trans. from German (1969); G.A. Mansuelli, *The Art of Etruria and Early Rome*, trans. from Italian (1965); Jocelyn M.C. Toynbee, *Art in Roman Britain* (1962); and Sir Mortimer Wheeler, *Roman Art and Architecture* (1964, reissued 1985). More detailed information on painting may be found in Amedeo Maiuri, *Roman Painting*, trans. from French (1953); and Wladimiro Dorigo, *Late Roman Painting* (1971; originally published in Italian, 1966). Bernard Andreae, *The Art of Rome* (1978; originally published in German, 1973), is a comprehensive survey; and Otto J. Brendel, *Prolegomena to the Study of Roman Art* (1979), includes criticism of previous writings on the subject.

EARLY CHRISTIAN, BYZANTINE, ARMENIAN, GEORGIAN, AND COPTIC

Viktor Lazarev, *Storia della pittura bizantina* (1967; originally published in Russian, 2 vol., 1947–48), is a well-annotated general survey, now seriously out of date but still useful. Good coverage is provided by a combination of two books: Beat Brenk (ed.), *Spätantike und frühes Christentum* (1977); and Wolfgang F.

Volbach and Jacqueline Lafontaine-Dosogne, *Byzanz und der christliche Osten* (1968). See also Wolfgang F. Volbach, *Early Christian Art*, with photographs by Max Hirmer (1962; originally published in German, 1958); and D. Talbot Rice, *Byzantine Art*, rev. ed. (1968); Thomas F. Mathews, *The Byzantine Churches of Istanbul: A Photographic Survey* (1976); and Cyril Mango, *The Art of the Byzantine Empire, 312–1453: Sources and Documents* (1972, reprinted 1986).

A number of books consider the art of the period as a whole and propose various ways of interpreting the material: André Grabar, *Christian Iconography: A Study of Its Origins* (1968, reprinted 1980; originally published in French, 1957; 2nd rev. French ed., 1984), *The Beginnings of Christian Art, 200–395* (1967; originally published in French, 1966), *Byzantium: From the Death of Theodosius to the Rise of Islam*, trans. from French (1967), and *Byzantine Painting: Historical and Critical Study*, trans. from French (1953, reissued 1979); Ernst Kitzinger, *Byzantine Art in the Making: Main Lines of Stylistic Development in Mediterranean Art, 3rd–7th Century* (1977); Clive Foss and Paul Magdalino, *Rome and Byzantium* (1977); and Cyril Mango, *Byzantium, the Empire of New Rome* (1980). Henry Maguire, *Art and Eloquence in Byzantium* (1981), discusses art as influenced by sermons and other theological writings; alternatively, Robin Cormack, *Writing in Gold: Byzantine Society and Its Icons* (1985), interprets Byzantine art as a major element in the Byzantine outlook.

A number of helpful publications cover some of the specialist areas: Klaus Wessel, *Coptic Art* (1965; originally published in German, 1963); Guiseppe Bovini, *Ravenna: Its Mosaics and Monuments* (1956, reissued 1970; originally published in Italian, 1956); Heinz Kähler, *Hagia Sophia* (1967; originally published in German, 1967); Anthony Bryerand Judith Herrin (eds.), *Iconoclasm* (1977); Kurt Weitzmann, *The Icon: Holy Images—Sixth to Fourteenth Century* (1978); and Kurt Weitzmann et al., *The Icon* (1982; originally published in Italian, 1981).

EARLY MEDIEVAL AND ROMANESQUE

The most satisfactory survey of the whole period is provided in André Grabar and Carl Nordenfalk, *Early Medieval Painting from the Fourth to the Eleventh Century*, trans. from French and German (1957), and *Romanesque Painting from the Eleventh to the Thirteenth Century*, trans. from French and German (1958). The most exhaustive study on wall painting is still Edgar W. Anthony, *Romanesque Frescoes* (1951, reprinted 1971). For manuscript illumination, see Albert Boeckler, *Abendländische Miniaturen bis zum Ausgang der romanischen Zeit* (1930); a stimulating discussion by Otto Pächt, *Book Illumination in the Middle Ages: An Introduction* (1986; originally published in German, 1984); and a survey by Christopher De Hamel, *A History of Illuminated Manuscripts* (1986). An excellent short introduction to the subject is contained in Ernst Kitzinger, *Early Medieval Art, with Illustrations from the British Museum and British Library Collections*, rev. ed. (1983). The 9th through 12th centuries are covered in John Beckwith, *Early Medieval Art: Carolingian, Ottonian, Romanesque*, rev. ed. (1969, reprinted 1985); and C.R. Dodwell, *Painting in Europe, 800 to 1200* (1971). The most comprehensive modern overview of Dark Age and early medieval painting is Carlo Bertelli, "Traccia allo studio delle fondazioni medievali dell'arte italiana," in *Storia dell'arte italiana*, part 2, *Dal medioevo al novecento*, vol. 1, *Dal medioevo al quattrocento*, pp. 3–163 (1983). For Rome, see Richard Krautheimer, *Rome, Profile of a City, 312–1308* (1980). The best survey of early Anglo-Saxon art is still T.D. Kendrick, *Anglo-Saxon Art to A.D. 900* (1938, reprinted 1972). For book illumination in Britain and Ireland, see J.J.G. Alexander, *Insular Manuscripts, 6th to the*

9th Century (1978); Carl Nordenfalk, *Celtic and Anglo-Saxon Painting: Book Illumination in the British Isles, 600–800* (1977); Françoise Henry, *Irish Art in the Early Christian Period, to 800 A.D.* (1965), *Irish Art During the Viking Invasions, 800–1020 A.D.* (1967), and *Irish Art in the Romanesque Period, 1020–1170 A.D.* (1970; originally published in French together in a set of 3 vol., 1963–64).

Merovingian illumination is discussed in Jean Hubert, Jean Porcher, and Wolfgang F. Volbach, *Europe in the Dark Ages* (1969; U.S. title, *Europe of the Invasions*; originally published in French, 1967). There are several good surveys of Carolingian painting: Wolfgang Braunfels, *Die Welt der Karolinger und ihre Kunst* (1968); Jean Hubert, Jean Porcher, and Wolfgang F. Volbach, *Carolingian Art* (1970; U.S. title, *The Carolingian Renaissance*; originally published in French, 1968); and Florentine Mütherich and Joachim E. Gaehde, *Carolingian Painting* (1976). Excellent particular studies can be found in Wolfgang Braunfels and Hermann Schnitzler (eds.), *Karolingische Kunst* (1965). Late Anglo-Saxon art is considered in Elzbieta Temple, *Anglo-Saxon Manuscripts, 900–1066* (1976); Janet Backhouse, D.H. Turner, and Leslie Webster (eds.), *The Golden Age of Anglo-Saxon Art, 966-1066* (1984); and C.R. Dodwell, *Anglo-Saxon Art: A New Perspective* (1982). Hans Jantzen, *Ottonische Kunst* (1947, reissued

1963), is an excellent review of Ottonian art; and Adolph Goldschmidt, *German Illumination, vol. 2, Ottonian Period* (1929, reprinted as part of a 1-vol. edition, 1970; originally published in German, 1928), is still valuable. A brief survey is Louis Grodecki et al., *Le Siècle de l'an mil* (1973). C.R. Dodwell and D.H. Turner, *Reichenau Reconsidered: A Re-assessment of the Place of Reichenau in Ottonian Art* (1965), offers a stimulating but contested examination of late 10th-century Ottonian illumination. The Romanesque period is surveyed in François Avril, *Xavier Barral I Altet*, and Danielle Gaborit-Chopin, *Le Temps des Croisades* (1982), and *Les Royaumes d'Occident* (1983); Hanns Swarzenski, *Monuments of Romanesque Art: The Art of Church Treasures in North-Western Europe*, 2nd ed. (1967, reissued 1974); Otto Demusand Max Hirmer, *Romanesque Mural Painting* (1970; originally published in German, 1968); and Walter Cahn, *Romanesque Bible Illumination* (1982). The best study of French Romanesque illumination is Jean Porcher, *Medieval French Miniatures* (1960; U.K. title, *French Miniatures from Illuminated Manuscripts*; originally published in French, 1959).

For England, there is an excellent survey of manuscripts: C.M. Kauffmann, *Romanesque Manuscripts, 1066–1190* (1975); and a later discussion in the exhibition catalog, George

Zarnecki, Janet Holt, and Tristram Holland (eds.), *English Romanesque Art, 1066–1200* (1984). The standard work on early Spanish illumination, in English, is J. Domínguez Bordona, *Spanish Illumination* (1930, reissued 1969; originally published in Spanish, 1930); see also John Williams, *Early Spanish Manuscript Illumination* (1977). Illumination in northwest Germany is surveyed in two exhibition catalogs, *Rhein und Maas, Kunst und Kultur, 800–1400,* 2 vol. (1972–73); and Anton Legner (ed.), *Ornamenta ecclesiae: Kunst und Künstler der Romanik,* 3 vol. (1985). The Gospels of Henry the Lion are discussed in *The Gospels of Henry the Lion, Count of Saxony, Duke of Bavaria* (1983), an auction catalog of Sotheby Parke Bernet Inc.; and Horst Fuhrmann and Florentine Mütherich (eds.), *Das Evangeliar Heinrichs des Löwen und das mittelalterliche Herrscherbild* (1986). The standard work on Salzburg illumination is still the masterly Georg Swarzenski, *Die Salzburger Malerei von den ersten Anfängen bis zur Blütezeit des romanischen Stils: Studien zur Geschichte der deutschen Malerei und Handschriftenkunde des Mittelalters,* 2nd ed., 2 vol. (1969). The best survey of the art of the late 12th century is found in the three volumes of *The Year 1200,* a set published in conjunction with an exhibition: vol. 1, *A Centennial*

Exhibition at the Metropolitan Museum of Art: A Catalog, edited by K. Hoffmann (1970); vol. 2, *A Background Survey*, edited by F. Deuchler (1970); and vol. 3, *A Symposium*, texts by François Avril et al. (1975). Otto Demus, *Byzantine Art and the West* (1970), discusses the influence of Byzantine art on western Europe throughout the Middle Ages.

GOTHIC

General social and intellectual studies of Gothic art include Joan Evans (ed.), *The Flowering of the Middle Ages*, new ed. (1985); and Johan Huizinga, *The Waning of the Middle Ages: A Study of the Forms of Life, Thought and Art in France and the Netherlands in the XIVth and XVth Centuries* (1924, reprinted 1985; originally published in Dutch, 1919). See also Andrew Martindale, *Gothic Art* (1967, reprinted 1985); George Henderson, *Early Medieval* (1972), and *Gothic* (1967); Emile Male, *Religious Art in France, the Thirteenth Century: A Study of Medieval Iconography and Its Sources* (1984; originally published in French, 9th rev. ed., 1958), and *Religious Art from the Twelfth to the Eighteenth Century* (1949, reprinted 1970; originally published in French, 1945); Teresa G. Frisch, *Gothic Art 1140–c. 1450*

(1971); and Jacques Dupont and Cesare Gnudi, *Gothic Painting* (1954, reissued 1979; originally published in French, 1954).

For a discussion of Italian Gothic painting, see Eve Borsook, *The Mural Painters of Tuscany: From Cimabue to Andrea del Sarto*, 2nd rev. ed. (1980); Millard Meiss, *Painting in Florence and Siena After the Black Death* (1951, reprinted 1978); John White, *Art and Architecture in Italy, 1250–1400* (1966), and *The Birth and Rebirth of Pictorial Space*, 2nd ed. (1967); and Frederick Antal, *Florentine Painting and Its Social Background: The Bourgeois Republic Before Cosimo de'Medici's Advent to Power, XIV and Early XV Centuries* (1948, reprinted 1986). Charles D. Cuttler, *Northern Painting from Pucelle to Bruegel: Fourteenth, Fifteenth, and Sixteenth Centuries* (1968), is an introductory work. No adequate monograph on International Gothic art exists, but, for France, see Millard Meiss, *French Painting in the Time of Jean de Berry: The Late Fourteenth Century and the Patronage of the Duke*, 2 vol. (1967), *French Painting in the Time of Jean de Berry: The Limbourgs and Their Contemporaries*, 2 vol. (1974), and *French Painting in the Time of Jean de Berry: The Boucicaut Master* (1968).

For late Gothic art, French painting is surveyed in Grete Ring, *A Century of French Painting, 1400–1500* (1949, reprinted 1979).

Netherlandish painting is dealt with in Max J. Friedländer, *Early Netherlandish Painting,* 14 vol. (1967–76; originally published in German, 1924–37); the best monograph on this early period is Erwin Panofsky, *Early Netherlandish Painting, Its Origins and Character,* 2 vol. (1953, reprinted 1971). Anne Shaver-Grandell, *The Middle Ages* (1982), is an introduction to medieval art intended for the general reader; Walter Oakeshott, *The Two Winchester Bibles* (1981), is a scholarly study of 12th-century painting; Richard I. Abrams and Warner A. Hutchinson, *An Illustrated Life of Jesus* (1982), includes an analysis of 94 paintings from the collection of the National Gallery of Art in Washington, D.C., with background notes on the artists; and Peter S. Beagle, *The Garden of Earthly Delights: Illustrations Taken from the Paintings of Hieronymus Bosch* (1982), is a creative and entertaining introduction to the artist's works.

RENAISSANCE

(Italy): General works include Creighton Gilbert, *History of Renaissance Art: Painting, Sculpture, Architecture Throughout Europe* (1973); Michael Levey, *Early Renaissance* (1967, reprinted 1979), and *High Renaissance*

(1975); and Robert Klein and Henri Zerner, *Italian Art, 1500–1600: Sources and Documents* (1966). A useful introduction to the theorists of the period is provided by Sir Anthony Blunt, *Artistic Theory in Italy, 1450–1600* (1940, reprinted 1982). See also Sydney J. Freedberg, *Painting of the High Renaissance in Rome and Florence*, new rev. ed., 2 vol. (1985), and *Painting in Italy, 1500 to 1600*, 2nd ed. (1983), a fine survey of the often-complex movements in 16th-century Italian painting; James Beck, *Italian Renaissance Painting* (1981), a historical survey of works of individual masters; and Bruce Cole, *The Renaissance Artist at Work: From Pisano to Titian* (1983).

(Northern Renaissance): Otto Benesch, *Art of the Renaissance in Northern Europe: Its Relation to the Contemporary Spiritual and Intellectual Movements*, rev. ed. (1965), and *German Painting, from Dürer to Holbein*, trans. from German (1966); Wolfgang Stechow, *Northern Renaissance Art, 1400–1600: Sources and Documents* (1966); and Albert Châtelet, *Early Dutch Painting: Painting in the Northern Netherlands in the Fifteenth Century* (1981; originally published in French, 1980). *(France)*: Sir Anthony Blunt, *Art and Architecture in France, 1500 to 1700*, 4th ed. (1980), is an authoritative survey. *(Spain and Portugal)*: George Kubler and Martin Soria, *Art and*

Architecture in Spain and Portugal and Their American Dominions, 1500 to 1800 (1959), is the only scholarly study in English. *(Central Europe and Russia)*: G.H. Hamilton, *The Art and Architecture of Russia*, 3rd ed. (1983), is a survey of all the arts of Russia.

Many studies have been done since the 1960s dealing exclusively with Mannerism. The most coherent view as a whole is John Shearman, *Mannerism* (1967). See also Franzsepp Würtenberger, *Mannerism: The European Style of the Sixteenth Century* (1963; originally published in German, 1962); and Giuliano Briganti, *Italian Mannerism* (1962; originally published in Italian, 1961).

BAROQUE AND ROCOCO

The classic study of Baroque art, Heinrich Wölfflin, *Renaissance and Baroque* (1964, reprinted 1984; originally published in German, 1888), remains an important basic study. Michael Kitson, *The Age of Baroque* (1966), provides an excellent modern summary. John Rupert Martin, *Baroque* (1977), is a fuller survey. Germain Bazin, *Baroque and Rococo*, trans. from French (1964, reprinted as *Baroque and Rococo Art*, 1974), covers the entire period in less detail, but it has in no way replaced the basic study by Fiske Kimball, *The Creation of the Rococo* (1943, reprinted as *The Creation of the Rococo Decorative Style*, 1980). Arno Schönberger and Halldor Soehner, *The Age of Rococo* (1960; U.S. title, *The Rococo Age: Art and Civilization of the 18th Century*; originally published in German, 1959), has excellent illustrations and detailed notes. Patronage during the period has been analyzed in depth by Francis Haskell, *Patrons and Painters: A Study in the Relations Between Italian Art and Society in the Age of the Baroque*, rev. ed. (1980). *(Italy)*: Denis Mahon, *Studies in Seicento Art and Theory* (1947, reprinted 1971), is of fundamental importance for an understanding of Baroque art in Italy. Rudolf Wittkower, *Art and Architecture in Italy, 1600 to 1750*, 3rd rev. ed. (1973, reprinted with corrections 1980), surveys the 17th century with clarity and includes a massive bibliography. Ellis Waterhouse, *Italian Baroque Painting*, 2nd ed. (1969), provides an introduction to the principal painters and stylistic movements of the time; a similar role is performed by Michael Levey, *Painting in Eighteenth-Century Venice*, 2nd rev. ed. (1980). *(Latin America)*: Pal Kelemen, *Baroque and Rococo in Latin America*, 2nd ed., 2 vol. (1967), is an introduction to the art of the 17th and 18th centuries, with an exhaustive bibliography.

(Flanders): The only comprehensive introduction to this period available in English is provided by Horst Gerson and E.H. ter Kuile, *Art and Architecture in Belgium, 1600 to 1800* (1960; originally published in German, 1942). (Holland): Jakob Rosenberg, Seymour Slive, and E.H. ter Kuile, *Dutch Art and Architecture, 1600 to 1800*, 3rd ed. (1977), provides an excellent survey of the period and a large bibliography; while Wolfgang Stechow, *Dutch Landscape Painting of the Seventeenth Century*, 2nd ed. (1968, reprinted 1981), is a particularly detailed and valuable study of this important facet of Dutch painting. Ingvar Bergström, *Dutch Still-Life Painting in the Seventeenth Century* (1956, reprinted 1983; originally published in Swedish, 1947), provides a survey of this group of paintings. *(France):* Important surveys are Wend Graf Kalnein and Michael Levey, *Art and Architecture of the Eighteenth Century in France* (1972); and Philip Conisbee, *Painting in Eighteenth-Century France* (1981). *(England)*: Ellis Waterhouse, *Painting in Britain, 1530 to 1790*, 4th ed. (1978); and Margaret Whinney and Oliver Millar, *English Art, 1625–1714* (1957), are both well-illustrated and include bibliographies. *(Central Europe)*: The best introduction to Baroque art in central Europe, available in English, is undoubtedly Eberhard Hempel,

Baroque Art and Architecture in Central Europe: Germany, Austria, Switzerland, Hungary, Czechoslovakia, Poland, trans. from German (1965). *(Scandinavia):* Most of the information available on Scandinavian art of the 17th and 18th centuries is to be found in museum and exhibition catalogs devoted to wider subjects, but the monograph by Gunnar W. Lundberg, *Roslin: Liv och verk,* 3 vol. in 2 (1957), is available, together with the relevant sections in Torben Holck Colding, *Aspects of Miniature Painting: Its Origins and Development* (1953).

NEOCLASSICISM, ROMANTICISM, AND REALISM

Important works on the period in general are Walter Friedlaender, *David to Delacroix,* trans. from German (1952, reprinted 1980); and Fritz Novotny, *Painting and Sculpture in Europe, 1780–1880,* 2nd ed. (1971, reissued 1980). Among the many general studies of Neoclassical art are Hugh Honour, *Neo-classicism* (1968, reprinted 1977), a sound introduction; Robert Rosenblum, *Transformations in Late Eighteenth Century Art* (1967), one of the best studies of the period; and David Irwin, *English Neoclassical Art: Studies in Inspiration and Taste* (1966), a book dealing exclusively with Neoclassical painting and sculpture in Britain. Among the most important works covering Romanticism are Marcel Brion, *Art of the Romantic Era: Romanticism, Classicism, Realism* (1966; originally published in French, 1963); Werner Hofmann, *The Earthly Paradise: Art in the Nineteenth Century* (1961; originally published in German, 1960); Francis D. Klingender, *Art and the Industrial Revolution*, rev. ed., edited by Arthur Elton (1968); Edgar P. Richardson, *The Way of Western Art, 1776–1914* (1939, reprinted 1969); Frederick Antal, *Classicism and Romanticism, with Other Studies in Art History* (1966); T.J. Clark, *The Absolute Bourgeois: Artists and Politics in France, 1848–1851* (1973, reprinted 1982), and *Image of the People: Gustave Courbet and the 1848 Revolution* (1973, reprinted 1982); Albert Boime, *The Academy and French Painting in the Nineteenth Century* (1971); Hugh Honour, *Romanticism* (1979); and Michel Le Bris, *Romantics and Romanticism*, trans. from French (1981). Linda Nochlin, *Realism and Tradition in Art, 1848–1900: Sources and Documents* (1966), and *Realism* (1971), are provocative studies. See also Barbara Novak, *American Painting of the Nineteenth Century: Realism, Idealism, and the American Experience*, 2nd ed. (1979), and *Art and Culture: American Landscape and Painting, 1825–1875* (2007).

MODERN

Among the numerous surveys of modern art are H.H. Arnason, *History of Modern Art: Painting, Sculpture, Architecture, Photography*, 7th rev. ed., updated by Daniel Wheeler (2012); Meyer Schapiro, *Modern Art* (2011); Clement Greenberg, *Art and Culture: Critical Essays* (2006); Harold Rosenberg, *The Tradition of the New* (1994); John Canaday, *Mainstreams of Modern Art*, 2nd ed. (1981); Jean Cassou, Emile Langui, and Nikolaus Pevsner, *Gateway to the Twentieth Century: Art and Culture in a Changing World* (1962); Sam Hunter, *American Art of the 20th Century: Painting, Sculpture, Architecture* (1973); Sam Hunter and John Jacobus, *Modern Art: Painting, Sculpture, Architecture*, 3rd rev. ed. (2000); and Robert L. Herbert (ed.), *Modern Artists on Art* (1964). See also Beverly Whitney Kean, *All the Empty Palaces: The Merchant Patrons of Modern Art in Pre-Revolutionary Russia* (1983), an original study of important developments in the history of European art; Siegfried Wichmann, *Japonisme: The Japanese Influence on Western Art in the 19th and 20th Centuries* (1981; originally published in German, 1980), a broad study including treatments of individual artists; and T.J. Clark, *The Painting of Modern Life: Paris in the Art of Manet and his Followers* (1984).

Important works dealing with modern painting include: Werner Haftmann, *Painting in the Twentieth Century*, 2nd ed., 2 vol. (1965; originally published in German, 1965); Bernard S. Myers, *Mexican Painting in Our Time* (1956); Guido Ballo, *Modern Italian Painting: From Futurism to the Present Day* (1958; originally published in Italian, 1956); and Alan Gowans, *The Restless Art: A History of Painters and Painting, 1760–1960* (1966). See also Paul Vogt, *Expressionism: German Painting, 1905–1920* (1980; originally published in German), and *Contemporary Painting* (1981; trans. from German), a survey of international painting mostly of the 1950s and 1960s; George H. Roeder, Jr., *Forum of Uncertainty: Confrontations with Modern Painting in Twentieth-Century American Thought* (1980); John Russell, *The Meanings of Modern Art*, rev. ed. (1981); Frank H. Goodyear, Jr., *Contemporary American Realism Since 1960* (1981); and Abraham A. Davidson, *Early American Modernist Painting, 1910–1935* (1981).

(Pre-Raphaelites): T.J. Baringer, et. al. *Pre-Raphaelites: Victorian Art and Design* (2013); Christopher Wood, *The Pre-Raphaelites* (1981); and *Pre-Raphaelites and Academics* (1981), a catalog of the exhibition organized in celebration of the publication of Wood's work. *(Impressionism and Postimpressionism)*: Linda Nochlin (ed.), *Impressionism and*

Post-Impressionism, 1874–1904: Sources and Documents (1966); Horst Keller, *Watercolors and Drawings of the French Impressionists and Their Parisian Contemporaries* (1982; originally published in German, 1980); John Rewald, *The History of Impressionism*, 4th rev. ed. (1973, reprinted 1980), and *Post-Impressionism, from van Gogh to Gauguin*, 3rd rev. ed. (1978). *(Fauvism)*: Georges Duthuit, *The Fauvist Painters* (1950; originally published in French, 1949). *(German Expressionism)*: Peter Selz, *German Expressionist Painting* (1957, reprinted 1974). *(Cubism)*: John Golding, *Cubism: A History and an Analysis, 1907–1914*, 2nd ed. (1968); Christopher Gray, *Cubist Aesthetic Theories* (1953); and Robert Rosenblum, *Cubism and Twentieth-Century Art*, rev. ed. (1966, reissued 1976). *(Futurism)*: Marianne W. Martin, *Futurist Art and Theory, 1909–1915* (1968, reprinted 1978). *(Suprematism and Constructivism)*: Camilla Gray, *The Russian Experiment in Art, 1863–1922*, rev. ed., edited by Marian Burleigh-Motley (1986). *(De Stijl and Neoplasticism)*: H.L.C. Jaffé, *De Stijl, 1917–1931: The Dutch Contribution to Modern Art* (1956, reprinted 1986); and Mildred Friedman (ed.), *De Stijl: Visions of Utopia* (1982), an exhibition catalog. *(Dada and Surrealism)*: Robert Motherwell (ed.), *The Dada Painters and Poets: An Anthology*, 2nd ed. (1981); Hans Richter, *Dada: Art and Anti-Art* (1966, reprinted 1978; originally published in German,

1964); William S. Rubin, *Dada, Surrealism, and Their Heritage* (1968, reprinted 1982); Patrick Waldberg, *Surrealism*, trans. from French (1962, reissued 1978); and Herbert S. Gershman, *The Surrealist Revolution in France* (1969, reprinted 1974). *(Abstract Expressionism)*: Barbara Rose, *American Art Since 1900*, rev. and expanded ed. (1975). *(Pop Art and Op Art)*: Mario Amaya, *Pop Art and After* (1965, reprinted 1972; U.K. title, *Pop as Art: A Survey of New Super Realism*); Lucy R. Lippard, *Pop Art* (1966); John Russell and Suzi Gablik (compilers), *Pop Art Redefined* (1969); Thomas E. Crow, *The Rise of the Sixties: American and European Art in the Era of Dissent* (2004); Alexander Dubadze and Suzanne Hudson, (eds.). *Contemporary Art: 1989 to the Present* (2013); Hal Foster and Rosalind Krauss, *Art Since 1900*, 2 vols (2011); and Kristine Stiles and Peter Selz, *Theories and Documents of Contemporary Art*, 2nd ed., (2012).

INDEX